JOB: SUFFERING AND THE GOD WHO SPEAKS

HE READS TRUTH

HE READS TRUTH

EXECUTIVE

**FOUNDER /
CHIEF EXECUTIVE OFFICER**
Raechel Myers

**CO-FOUNDER /
CHIEF CONTENT OFFICER**
Amanda Bible Williams

**CHIEF OPERATING OFFICER /
CREATIVE DIRECTOR**
Ryan Myers

EXECUTIVE ASSISTANT
Catherine Cromer

EDITORIAL

CONTENT DIRECTOR
John Greco, MDiv

MANAGING EDITOR
Jessica Lamb

KIDS READ TRUTH EDITOR
Melanie Rainer, MATS

CONTENT EDITOR
Kara Gause

EDITORIAL ASSISTANT
Ellen Taylor

MARKETING

MARKETING MANAGER
Kayla Stinson

SOCIAL MEDIA STRATEGIST
Ansley Rushing

COMMUNITY SUPPORT SPECIALIST
Margot Williams

CREATIVE

ART DIRECTOR
Amanda Barnhart

DESIGNERS
Brandon Triola
Kelsea Allen

ARTIST-IN-RESIDENCE
Emily Knapp

JUNIOR DESIGNER
Abbey Benson

SHIPPING & LOGISTICS

LOGISTICS MANAGER
Lauren Gloyne

SHIPPING MANAGER
Sydney Bess

FULFILLMENT COORDINATOR
Katy McKnight

FULFILLMENT SPECIALIST
Julia Rogers

SUBSCRIPTION INQUIRIES
orders@hereadstruth.com

COLOPHON

This book was printed offset in Nashville, Tennessee, on 60# Lynx Opaque Text under the direction of He Reads Truth. The cover is 100# Lynx Opaque Cover with a soft touch aqueous coating.

COPYRIGHT

© 2019 by He Reads Truth, LLC
All rights reserved.

All photography used by permission.

ISBN 978-1-949526-17-2

No part of this publication may be reproduced, distributed, or transmitted in any form or by any means, including photocopying, recording, or other electronic or mechanical methods, without the prior written permission of He Reads Truth, LLC, except in the case of brief quotations embodied in critical reviews and certain other noncommercial uses permitted by copyright law.

Unless otherwise noted, all Scripture is taken from the Christian Standard Bible®. Copyright © 2017 by Holman Bible Publishers. Used by permission. Christian Standard Bible® and CSB® are federally registered trademarks of Holman Bible Publishers.

Research support provided by Logos Bible Software™. Learn more at logos.com.

@hereadstruth   hereadstruth.com

EDITOR'S LETTER

Suffering reminds us that something has gone terribly wrong in our world and that we were meant for another—one without heartache, tears, or death. Beauty offers us a preview of that world, which is our true home. The book of Job is a collision of suffering and beauty. As literature, it is a work of art, an epic poem of the first order, set in cycles of dialogue that rival any masterpiece from antiquity. But the subject matter of Job is anything but light.

Job is a righteous man, blessed by God, and has seen more goodness in his life than pain, until he loses everything: his possessions, his family, his health. For most of the book, Job resigns himself to the ash heaps of the town dump, scratching the open sores that cover his body with a piece of broken pottery (2:8). He has lost everything, and the unrelenting question that fills his mind is, *Why?*

Though Job's case is extreme, I believe we are meant to see ourselves in his story. No one is immune from suffering. No one escapes life unscathed.

When our editorial team sat down to discuss how we might approach the book of Job, we felt the weight of knowing this book has been one of the most requested by our community. There are a lot of people, like Job, asking *Why?* But the more we pored over our open Bibles and talked, the more we realized that Job is never given a reason for his suffering. When the book ends, he's hasn't been told about the scenes that took place behind the veil separating the earthly realm from the heavenly one. He's not given an answer to his *Why*. What Job gets is something far better. He gets God Himself.

The God who commands the morning, who provides food for the ravens, and who leads the stars in their path across the sky (38:12, 41, 32) is also the God who speaks to His children. Hope in suffering does not come from figuring out why bad things happen. It comes from knowing God is right there, with us, in the midst of our pain.

The extras in this legacy book are designed to help you reflect on the story of Job, to engage your heart as well as your mind. As you read through this plan in the coming weeks, my prayer is that you will hear God speak to you through His Word and that the peace you find in every dark season will be the Redeemer who lives, Christ Jesus (19:25).

For His kingdom,

John Greco

JOHN GRECO
CONTENT DIRECTOR

DESIGN ON PURPOSE

We chose black as the primary color for this book to reflect the suffering Job endured. This dark color also reflects Job's struggle as he searched for a reason for his pain.

The running horizontal line throughout the book represents the silence of God as Job argued about his suffering with his friends. On Grace Days and in the final chapters of Job, the line transitions to an icon of sound waves as a representation of the power and truth found in God's voice.

THE HE READS TRUTH CREATIVE TEAM

HOW TO USE THIS BOOK

Each book in the He Reads Truth Legacy Series™ provides space to read and study Scripture, make notes, and record prayers. As you build your library, you will have a record of your Bible-reading journey to reference and pass down.

SCRIPTURE READING PLAN

Designed for a Monday start, this Legacy Book presents the book of Job in daily readings, plus supplemental passages for additional context.

RESPONSE

Each daily reading closes with space for notes and prayers.

GRACE DAY

Use Saturdays to pray, rest, and reflect on what you've read.

WEEKLY TRUTH

Sundays are set aside for weekly Scripture memorization.

Find corresponding memory cards in the back of this book.

EXTRAS

This book features additional tools to help you gain a deeper understanding of the text.

For added community and conversation, join us in the **Job** reading plan on the He Reads Truth™ app or at HeReadsTruth.com.

Table of Contents

WEEK 1	DAY 1	THE SETTING OF THE TEST	18
	DAY 2	JOB'S LAMENT	24
	DAY 3	ELIPHAZ'S FIRST SPEECH	28
	DAY 4	JOB'S REPLY TO ELIPHAZ	32
	DAY 5	BILDAD'S FIRST SPEECH AND JOB'S REPLY	38
	DAY 6	GRACE DAY	44
	DAY 7	WEEKLY TRUTH	46

WEEK 2	DAY 8	ZOPHAR'S FIRST SPEECH AND JOB'S REPLY	48
	DAY 9	JOB CHALLENGES THE ADVICE OF HIS FRIENDS	56
	DAY 10	ELIPHAZ'S SECOND SPEECH AND JOB'S REPLY	60
	DAY 11	BILDAD'S SECOND SPEECH AND JOB'S REPLY	66
	DAY 12	ZOPHAR'S SECOND SPEECH AND JOB'S REPLY	72
	DAY 13	GRACE DAY	78
	DAY 14	WEEKLY TRUTH	80

WEEK 3	DAY 15	ELIPHAZ'S THIRD SPEECH AND JOB'S REPLY	82
	DAY 16	BILDAD'S THIRD SPEECH AND JOB'S REPLY	88
	DAY 17	WHERE IS WISDOM FOUND?	92
	DAY 18	JOB SPEAKS ABOUT HIS CONDITION	98
	DAY 19	ELIHU SPEAKS TO JOB'S CONDITION	104
	DAY 20	GRACE DAY	110
	DAY 21	WEEKLY TRUTH	112

WEEK 4	DAY 22	ELIHU'S APPEAL TO WISDOM	114
	DAY 23	THE MERCY AND MAJESTY OF GOD	120
	DAY 24	GOD'S FIRST SPEECH	126
	DAY 25	GOD'S SECOND SPEECH	134
	DAY 26	THE RESTORATION OF JOB	140
	DAY 27	GRACE DAY	144
	DAY 28	WEEKLY TRUTH	146

Extras	WISDOM LITERATURE IN SCRIPTURE	12
	JOB'S COUNSELORS	52
	TRIALS OF MANY KINDS	96
	ASKED IN JOB, ANSWERED IN JESUS	132
	STUDY QUESTIONS	148

God whispers to us in in our conscience, but it is His megaphone

our pleasures, speaks
shouts in our pains:
to rouse a deaf world.

C.S. Lewis

Wisdom Literature in Scripture

What does it mean to live a life that is pleasing to God? The books of Job, Proverbs, and Ecclesiastes each wrestle with this question in different ways. Proverbs lays the foundation for biblical wisdom, while Job and Ecclesiastes focus on unexpected circumstances in life. Together, all three of these books offer a distinct but unified view of what it means to live out the wisdom of God.

01 PROVERBS

The fear of the Lord is the beginning of knowledge; fools despise wisdom and discipline. PR 1:7

- A collection of traditional wisdom. Contains many common-sense sayings and a few extended wisdom poems. Meant to be read as general rules, not absolute promises.

- The book of Proverbs offers positive and negative principles for living in the world God created, emphasizing "fear of the Lord" as the source of all wisdom and the connection between character and consequences.

02 ECCLESIASTES

When all has been heard, the conclusion of the matter is this: fear God and keep his commands, because this is for all humanity. EC 12:13

- A mixture of poetry and prose.

- Ecclesiastes observes that following wisdom doesn't always guarantee a positive outcome. Difficulties in life defy simple explanation, and the author wrestles with this existential tension. He concludes our ultimate purpose is to "fear God and keep his commands."

03 JOB

But I know that my Redeemer lives, and at the end he will stand on the dust. JB 19:25

- A narrative prologue and epilogue, with poetic dialogues between Job and his friends making up most of the book. Eliphaz, Bildad, Zophar, and Elihu each attempt to apply traditional wisdom to Job's situation.

- The book of Job provides spiritual insight for the problem of suffering. God is wise and powerful, even in our darkest seasons.

BUT I KNOW THAT MY REDEEMER LIVES, AND AT THE END HE WILL STAND ON THE DUST. **JOB 19:25**

ON THE TIMELINE

Although Job is set in the patriarchal period, its date of writing and author are unknown. Jewish tradition places the writing of Job during the time of Moses, around 1440 BC.

A LITTLE BACKGROUND

In Job's era, wealth was measured in cattle and servants. Like other Old Testament patriarchal family heads, Job performed priestly duties, including offering sacrifices for his family. And like the patriarchs, Job lived to be more than one hundred years old (42:16). Geographically, the events took place in the northern Arabian Peninsula, in the land of Uz (1:1), often associated with Edom.

MESSAGE & PURPOSE

The book of Job demonstrates that a sovereign, righteous God is sufficient and trustworthy for every situation in life, even in the most difficult of circumstances. Along with this truth, Job portrays other additional themes:

- *Character*—Job is introduced as a man of character (1:1), and God testified to his consistently blameless character (1:8; 2:3). As Job saw it, in God's dealings with man, God does not appear to always reward a blameless and pure life (9:23; 10:14).

- *Righteousness*—Job stated that his righteousness was the central issue in his situation (6:29), yet he wondered how he could convince God of this (9:2, 15, 20; 10:15). All three of Job's friends condemned Job's attitude as self-righteous (32:1).

- *Justice*—Job wanted to receive justice in his situation (19:7; 23:4). He renounced injustice (27:4) and modeled justice in his dealings with others (29:14; 31:13-15). Job felt that God had not always dealt justly with him (14:3; 23:10-16; 34:5-6). Rather than championing his own righteousness, Job was called to understand God's essential righteousness by which He justly governs the universe (40:7-14).

GIVE THANKS FOR THE BOOK OF JOB

In the book of Job we are reminded that suffering comes to everyone, the righteous and unrighteous alike. God does not always keep the righteous from danger or suffering. Ultimately, God controls all of life's situations. The book of Job demonstrates poignantly that God's comfort and strength are always available to the trusting soul.

OUTLINE OF JOB

I. PROLOGUE:

THE SETTING OF THE TEST
1:1-2:13

A. Job's life before the test (1:1-5)
B. Satan's first accusation and proposed test (1:6-12)
C. Job's response to the first test (1:13-22)
D. Satan's second accusation and proposed test (2:1-7)
E. Job's response to the second test (2:8-10)
F. The arrival of Job's comforters (2:11-13)

II. DEVELOPMENT:

EXAMINING JOB'S CONDITION
3:1-27:23

A. Job's lament over his condition (3:1-26)
B. Dialogues about Job's condition (4:1-27:23)

III. CLIMAX:

EXPLAINING JOB'S CONDITION
28:1-37:4

A. Job's speeches about his condition (28:1-31:40)
B. Elihu's speeches about Job's condition (32:1-42:6)

IV. RESOLUTION:

JOB'S CONDITION AND GOD'S GREATNESS
38:1-42:6

A. God's first speech: his sovereign power (38:1-40:2)
B. Job's response: his self-renunciation (40:3-5)
C. God's second speech: Job's impotence (40:6-41:34)
D. Job's response: his repentance (42:1-6)

V. EPILOGUE:

THE SCENE AFTER THE TEST
42:7-17

A. Job and his comforters (42:7-9)
B. Job and his family (42:10-17)

Day 1

THE SETTING OF THE TEST

JOB 1–2, PSALM 22:1–11

JOB 1

JOB AND HIS FAMILY

¹ There was a man in the country of Uz named Job. He was a man of complete integrity, who feared God and turned away from evil. ² He had seven sons and three daughters. ³ His estate included seven thousand sheep and goats, three thousand camels, five hundred yoke of oxen, five hundred female donkeys, and a very large number of servants. Job was the greatest man among all the people of the east.

⁴ His sons used to take turns having banquets at their homes. They would send an invitation to their three sisters to eat and drink with them. ⁵ Whenever a round of banqueting was over, Job would send for his children and purify them, rising early in the morning to offer burnt offerings for all of them. For Job thought, "Perhaps my children have sinned, having cursed God in their hearts." This was Job's regular practice.

SATAN'S FIRST TEST OF JOB

⁶ One day the sons of God came to present themselves before the LORD, and Satan also came with them. ⁷ The LORD asked Satan, "Where have you come from?"

"From roaming through the earth," Satan answered him, "and walking around on it."

⁸ Then the LORD said to Satan, "Have you considered my servant Job? No one else on earth is like him, a man of perfect integrity, who fears God and turns away from evil."

⁹ Satan answered the LORD, "Does Job fear God for nothing? ¹⁰ Haven't you placed a hedge around him, his household, and everything he owns? You have blessed the work of his hands, and his possessions have increased in the land. ¹¹ But stretch out your hand and strike everything he owns, and he will surely curse you to your face."

¹² "Very well," the LORD told Satan, "everything he owns is in your power. However, do not lay a hand on Job himself." So Satan left the LORD's presence.

¹³ One day when Job's sons and daughters were eating and drinking wine in their oldest brother's house, ¹⁴ a messenger came to Job and reported: "While

the oxen were plowing and the donkeys grazing nearby, [15] the Sabeans swooped down and took them away. They struck down the servants with the sword, and I alone have escaped to tell you!"

[16] He was still speaking when another messenger came and reported: "God's fire fell from heaven. It burned the sheep and the servants and devoured them, and I alone have escaped to tell you!"

[17] That messenger was still speaking when yet another came and reported: "The Chaldeans formed three bands, made a raid on the camels, and took them away. They struck down the servants with the sword, and I alone have escaped to tell you!"

[18] He was still speaking when another messenger came and reported: "Your sons and daughters were eating and drinking wine in their oldest brother's house. [19] Suddenly a powerful wind swept in from the desert and struck the four corners of the house. It collapsed on the young people so that they died, and I alone have escaped to tell you!"

[20] Then Job stood up, tore his robe, and shaved his head. He fell to the ground and worshiped, [21] saying:

> Naked I came from my mother's womb,
> and naked I will leave this life.
> The Lord gives, and the Lord takes away.
> Blessed be the name of the Lord.

[22] Throughout all this Job did not sin or blame God for anything.

JOB 2

SATAN'S SECOND TEST OF JOB

[1] One day the sons of God came again to present themselves before the Lord, and Satan also came with them to present himself before the Lord. [2] The Lord asked Satan, "Where have you come from?"

"From roaming through the earth," Satan answered him, "and walking around on it."

³ Then the Lord said to Satan, "Have you considered my servant Job? No one else on earth is like him, a man of perfect integrity, who fears God and turns away from evil. He still retains his integrity, even though you incited me against him, to destroy him for no good reason."
⁴ "Skin for skin!" Satan answered the Lord. "A man will give up everything he owns in exchange for his life. ⁵ But stretch out your hand and strike his flesh and bones, and he will surely curse you to your face."

⁶ "Very well," the Lord told Satan, "he is in your power; only spare his life."
⁷ So Satan left the Lord's presence and infected Job with terrible boils from the soles of his feet to the top of his head. ⁸ Then Job took a piece of broken pottery to scrape himself while he sat among the ashes.

⁹ His wife said to him, "Are you still holding on to your integrity? Curse God and die!"

¹⁰ "You speak as a foolish woman speaks," he told her.

"Should we accept only good from God and not adversity?"

Throughout all this Job did not sin in what he said.

JOB'S THREE FRIENDS

¹¹ Now when Job's three friends—Eliphaz the Temanite, Bildad the Shuhite, and Zophar the Naamathite—heard about all this adversity that had happened to him, each of them came from his home. They met together to go and sympathize with him and comfort him. ¹² When they looked from a distance, they could barely recognize him. They wept aloud, and each man tore his robe and threw dust into the air and on his head. ¹³ Then they sat on the ground with him seven days and nights, but no one spoke a word to him because they saw that his suffering was very intense.

PSALM 22:1-11

FROM SUFFERING TO PRAISE

For the choir director: according to "The Deer of the Dawn." A psalm of David.

¹ My God, my God, why have you abandoned me?
Why are you so far from my deliverance
and from my words of groaning?
² My God, I cry by day, but you do not answer,
by night, yet I have no rest.
³ But you are holy,
enthroned on the praises of Israel.
⁴ Our fathers trusted in you;
they trusted, and you rescued them.
⁵ They cried to you and were set free;
they trusted in you and were not disgraced.

⁶ But I am a worm and not a man,
scorned by mankind and despised by people.
⁷ Everyone who sees me mocks me;
they sneer and shake their heads:
⁸ "He relies on the LORD;
let him save him;
let the LORD rescue him,
since he takes pleasure in him."

⁹ It was you who brought me out of the womb,
making me secure at my mother's breast.
¹⁰ I was given over to you at birth;
you have been my God from my mother's womb.

¹¹ Don't be far from me, because distress is near
and there's no one to help.

NOTES

Job - Man of God, turns from evil.
Perfect integrity - being honest, having strong
moral principles and uprightness. No one on
earth like him.

Because of this he is blessed by God

Even through adversity, he still worships God.

We need people to walk with us when
we face challenging situations in life.

"There is hope for the helpless. Rest for
the weary. And love for the broken heart.
And there is grace and forgiveness, Mercy
and healing. He'll meet you wherever
you are. Cry out to Jesus. Cry out to
Jesus." - Cry out to Jesus, Third Day

"My God. I cry by day, but you do
not answer. By night. yet I have
no rest." Psalm 22:2
↳ Why? this is so tough. Is it
because God's timing is perfect?

Day 2

JOB'S LAMENT

JOB 3, PHILIPPIANS 3:7–11, 2 TIMOTHY 2:8–13

JOB 3

JOB'S OPENING SPEECH

¹ After this, Job began to speak and cursed the day he was born. ² He said:

> ³ May the day I was born perish,
> and the night that said,
> "A boy is conceived."
> ⁴ If only that day had turned to darkness!
> May God above not care about it,
> or light shine on it.
> ⁵ May darkness and gloom reclaim it,
> and a cloud settle over it.
> May what darkens the day terrify it.
> ⁶ If only darkness had taken that night away!
> May it not appear among the days of the year
> or be listed in the calendar.
> ⁷ Yes, may that night be barren;
> may no joyful shout be heard in it.
> ⁸ Let those who curse days
> condemn it,
> those who are ready to rouse Leviathan.
> ⁹ May its morning stars grow dark.
> May it wait for daylight but have none;
> may it not see the breaking of dawn.
> ¹⁰ For that night did not shut
> the doors of my mother's womb,
> and hide sorrow from my eyes.
>
> ¹¹ Why was I not stillborn;
> why didn't I die as I came from the womb?
> ¹² Why did the knees receive me,
> and why were there breasts for me to nurse?
> ¹³ Now I would certainly be lying down in peace;
> I would be asleep.
> Then I would be at rest
> ¹⁴ with the kings and counselors of the earth,
> who rebuilt ruined cities for themselves,
> ¹⁵ or with princes who had gold,
> who filled their houses with silver.
> ¹⁶ Or why was I not hidden like a miscarried child,
> like infants who never see daylight?

[17] There the wicked cease to make trouble,
and there the weary find rest.
[18] The captives are completely at rest;
they do not hear a taskmaster's voice.
[19] Both small and great are there,
and the slave is set free from his master.

[20] Why is light given to one burdened with grief,
and life to those whose existence is bitter,
[21] who wait for death, but it does not come,
and search for it more than for hidden treasure,
[22] who are filled with much joy
and are glad when they reach the grave?
[23] Why is life given to a man whose path is hidden,
whom God has hedged in?
[24] I sigh when food is put before me,
and my groans pour out like water.
[25] For the thing I feared has overtaken me,
and what I dreaded has happened to me.
[26] I cannot relax or be calm;
I have no rest, for turmoil has come.

PHILIPPIANS 3:7-11

[7] But everything that was a gain to me, I have considered to be a loss because of Christ. [8] More than that, I also consider everything to be a loss in view of the surpassing value of knowing Christ Jesus my Lord. Because of him I have suffered the loss of all things and consider them as dung, so that I may gain Christ [9] and be found in him, not having a righteousness of my own from the law, but one that is through faith in Christ—the righteousness from God based on faith.

[10] My goal is to know him and the power of his resurrection and the fellowship of his sufferings, being conformed to his death,

[11] assuming that I will somehow reach the resurrection from among the dead.

we will also live with him;

¹² if we endure, we will also reign with him;
if we deny him, he will also deny us;

¹³ if we are faithless, he remains faithful,
for he cannot deny himself.

NOTES

Job curses the day he was born. Hardship causes us to put our full trust in God. We give up those things that are valuable in human eyes in order to receive God's blessings.

"My old self has been crucified w/ Christ. It is no longer I who live but Christ who lives in me." — Galatians 2:20

He is still faithful when we are faithless.

"Three things will last forever — Faith, Hope & Love — and the greatest of these is love."
— 1 Corinthians 13:13

Day 3

ELIPHAZ'S FIRST SPEECH

JOB 4–5, ROMANS 5:1, 1 CORINTHIANS 3:18–23

JOB 4

FIRST SERIES OF SPEECHES

ELIPHAZ SPEAKS

[1] Then Eliphaz the Temanite replied:

[2] Should anyone try to speak with you
when you are exhausted?
Yet who can keep from speaking?
[3] Indeed, you have instructed many
and have strengthened weak hands.
[4] Your words have steadied the one who
    was stumbling
and braced the knees that were buckling.
[5] But now that this has happened to you,
you have become exhausted.
It strikes you, and you are dismayed.
[6] Isn't your piety your confidence,
and the integrity of your life your hope?
[7] Consider: Who has perished when he
    was innocent?
Where have the honest been destroyed?
[8] In my experience, those who plow injustice
and those who sow trouble reap the same.
[9] They perish at a single blast from God
and come to an end by the breath of
    his nostrils.
[10] The lion may roar and the fierce lion growl,
but the teeth of young lions are broken.
[11] The strong lion dies if it catches no prey,
and the cubs of the lioness are scattered.

[12] A word was brought to me in secret;
my ears caught a whisper of it.
[13] Among unsettling thoughts from visions
    in the night,
when deep sleep comes over men,
[14] fear and trembling came over me
and made all my bones shake.
[15] I felt a draft on my face,
and the hair on my body stood up.

[16] A figure stood there,
but I could not recognize its appearance;
a form loomed before my eyes.
I heard a whispering voice:
[17] "Can a mortal be righteous before God?
Can a man be more pure than his Maker?"
[18] If God puts no trust in his servants
and he charges his angels with foolishness,
[19] how much more those who dwell in
    clay houses,
whose foundation is in the dust,
who are crushed like a moth!
[20] They are smashed to pieces from dawn
    to dusk;
they perish forever while no one notices.
[21] Are their tent cords not pulled up?
They die without wisdom.

JOB 5

[1] Call out! Will anyone answer you?
Which of the holy ones will you turn to?
[2] For anger kills a fool,
and jealousy slays the gullible.
[3] I have seen a fool taking root,
but I immediately pronounced a curse on
    his home.
[4] His children are far from safety.
They are crushed at the city gate,
with no one to rescue them.
[5] The hungry consume his harvest,
even taking it out of the thorns.
The thirsty pant for his children's wealth.
[6] For distress does not grow out of the soil,
and trouble does not sprout from the ground.
[7] But humans are born for trouble
as surely as sparks fly upward.

⁸ However, if I were you, I would appeal to God
and would present my case to him.
⁹ He does great and unsearchable things,
wonders without number.
¹⁰ He gives rain to the earth
and sends water to the fields.
¹¹ He sets the lowly on high,
and mourners are lifted to safety.
¹² He frustrates the schemes of the crafty
so that they achieve no success.
¹³ He traps the wise in their craftiness
so that the plans of the deceptive
are quickly brought to an end.
¹⁴ They encounter darkness by day,
and they grope at noon
as if it were night.
¹⁵ He saves the needy from their sharp words
and from the clutches of the powerful.
¹⁶ So the poor have hope,
and injustice shuts its mouth.
¹⁷ See how happy is the person whom God corrects;
so do not reject the discipline of the Almighty.
¹⁸ For he wounds but he also bandages;
he strikes, but his hands also heal.
¹⁹ He will rescue you from six calamities;
no harm will touch you in seven.
²⁰ In famine he will redeem you from death,
and in battle, from the power of the sword.
²¹ You will be safe from slander
and not fear destruction when it comes.
²² You will laugh at destruction and hunger
and not fear the land's wild creatures.
²³ For you will have a covenant with the stones of the field,
and the wild animals will be at peace with you.
²⁴ You will know that your tent is secure,
and nothing will be missing when you inspect your home.
²⁵ You will also know that your offspring will be many
and your descendants like the grass of the earth.
²⁶ You will approach the grave in full vigor,
as a stack of sheaves is gathered in its season.
²⁷ We have investigated this, and it is true!
Hear it and understand it for yourself.

ROMANS 5:1

Therefore, since we have been declared righteous by faith, we have peace with God through our Lord Jesus Christ.

1 CORINTHIANS 3:18-23

THE FOLLY OF HUMAN WISDOM

[18] Let no one deceive himself. If anyone among you thinks he is wise in this age, let him become a fool so that he can become wise. [19] For the wisdom of this world is foolishness with God, since it is written, He catches the wise in their craftiness; [20] and again, The Lord knows that the reasonings of the wise are futile. [21] So let no one boast in human leaders, for everything is yours—[22] whether Paul or Apollos or Cephas or the world or life or death or things present or things to come—everything is yours, [23] and you belong to Christ, and Christ belongs to God.

NOTES

We belong to christ and Christ belongs to God. We have peace with God through Christ. Is it prideful to believe you are wise?

Day 4

JOB'S REPLY TO ELIPHAZ

JOB 6–7, ROMANS 8:18–25

JOB 6

JOB'S REPLY TO ELIPHAZ

¹ Then Job answered:

² If only my grief could be weighed
and my devastation placed with it on the scales.
³ For then it would outweigh the sand of the seas!
That is why my words are rash.
⁴ Surely the arrows of the Almighty have pierced me;
my spirit drinks their poison.
God's terrors are arrayed against me.
⁵ Does a wild donkey bray over fresh grass
or an ox low over its fodder?
⁶ Is bland food eaten without salt?
Is there flavor in an egg white?
⁷ I refuse to touch them;
they are like contaminated food.

⁸ If only my request would be granted
and God would provide what I hope for:
⁹ that he would decide to crush me,
to unleash his power and cut me off!
¹⁰ It would still bring me comfort,
and I would leap for joy in unrelenting pain
that I have not denied the words of the Holy One.

¹¹ What strength do I have, that I should continue to hope?
What is my future, that I should be patient?
¹² Is my strength that of stone,
or my flesh made of bronze?
¹³ Since I cannot help myself,
the hope for success has been banished from me.

¹⁴ A despairing man should receive loyalty from his friends,
even if he abandons the fear of the Almighty.
¹⁵ My brothers are as treacherous as a wadi,
as seasonal streams that overflow
¹⁶ and become darkened because of ice,
and the snow melts into them.
¹⁷ The wadis evaporate in warm weather;
they disappear from their channels in hot weather.

¹⁸ Caravans turn away from their routes,
go up into the desert, and perish.
¹⁹ The caravans of Tema look for these streams.
The traveling merchants of Sheba hope for them.
²⁰ They are ashamed because they had been confident of finding water.
When they arrive there, they are disappointed.
²¹ So this is what you have now become to me.
When you see something dreadful, you are afraid.
²² Have I ever said: "Give me something"
or "Pay a bribe for me from your wealth"
²³ or "Deliver me from the enemy's hand"
or "Redeem me from the hand of the ruthless"?

²⁴ Teach me, and I will be silent.
Help me understand what I did wrong.
²⁵ How painful honest words can be!
But what does your rebuke prove?
²⁶ Do you think that you can disprove my words
or that a despairing man's words are mere wind?
²⁷ No doubt you would cast lots for a fatherless child
and negotiate a price to sell your friend.

²⁸ But now, please look at me;
I will not lie to your face.
²⁹ Reconsider; don't be unjust.
Reconsider; my righteousness is still the issue.
³⁰ Is there injustice on my tongue
or can my palate not taste disaster?

JOB 7

¹ Isn't each person consigned to forced labor on earth?
Are not his days like those of a hired worker?
² Like a slave he longs for shade;
like a hired worker he waits for his pay.
³ So I have been made to inherit months of futility,
and troubled nights have been assigned to me.
⁴ When I lie down I think,
"When will I get up?"
But the evening drags on endlessly,
and I toss and turn until dawn.

⁵ My flesh is clothed with maggots and encrusted with dirt.
My skin forms scabs and then oozes.

⁶ My days pass more swiftly than a weaver's shuttle;
they come to an end without hope.
⁷ Remember that my life is but a breath.
My eye will never again see anything good.
⁸ The eye of anyone who looks on me
will no longer see me.
Your eyes will look for me, but I will be gone.
⁹ As a cloud fades away and vanishes,
so the one who goes down to Sheol will never rise again.
¹⁰ He will never return to his house;
his hometown will no longer remember him.

¹¹ Therefore I will not restrain my mouth.
I will speak in the anguish of my spirit;
I will complain in the bitterness of my soul.
¹² Am I the sea or a sea monster,
that you keep me under guard?
¹³ When I say, "My bed will comfort me,
and my couch will ease my complaint,"
¹⁴ then you frighten me with dreams,
and terrify me with visions,
¹⁵ so that I prefer strangling—
death rather than life in this body.
¹⁶ I give up! I will not live forever.
Leave me alone, for my days are a breath.

¹⁷ What is a mere human, that you think so highly of him
and pay so much attention to him?
¹⁸ You inspect him every morning,
and put him to the test every moment.
¹⁹ Will you ever look away from me,
or leave me alone long enough to swallow?
²⁰ If I have sinned, what have I done to you,
Watcher of humanity?
Why have you made me your target,
so that I have become a burden to you?
²¹ Why not forgive my sin
and pardon my iniquity?

For soon I will lie down in the grave.
You will eagerly seek me, but I will be gone.

ROMANS 8:18-25

FROM GROANS TO GLORY

[18] For I consider that the sufferings of this present time are not worth comparing with the glory that is going to be revealed to us. [19] For the creation eagerly waits with anticipation for God's sons to be revealed. [20] For the creation was subjected to futility—not willingly, but because of him who subjected it—in the hope [21] that the creation itself will also be set free from the bondage to decay into the glorious freedom of God's children. [22] For we know that the whole creation has been groaning together with labor pains until now.

[23] Not only that, but we ourselves who have the Spirit as the firstfruits—we also groan within ourselves, eagerly waiting for adoption, the redemption of our bodies.

[24] Now in this hope we were saved, but hope that is seen is not hope, because who hopes for what he sees? [25] Now if we hope for what we do not see, we eagerly wait for it with patience.

NOTES

Day 5

BILDAD'S FIRST SPEECH AND JOB'S REPLY

JOB 8–10, NAHUM 1:3, ROMANS 3:23–26

JOB 8

BILDAD SPEAKS

¹ Then Bildad the Shuhite replied:

² How long will you go on saying
   these things?
Your words are a blast of wind.
³ Does God pervert justice?
Does the Almighty pervert what is right?
⁴ Since your children sinned against him,
he gave them over to their rebellion.
⁵ But if you earnestly seek God
and ask the Almighty for mercy,
⁶ if you are pure and upright,
then he will move even now on your behalf
and restore the home where your
   righteousness dwells.
⁷ Then, even if your beginnings were modest,
your final days will be full of prosperity.

⁸ For ask the previous generation,
and pay attention to what their
   fathers discovered,
⁹ since we were born only yesterday and
   know nothing.
Our days on earth are but a shadow.
¹⁰ Will they not teach you and tell you
and speak from their understanding?
¹¹ Does papyrus grow where there is
   no marsh?
Do reeds flourish without water?
¹² While still uncut shoots,
they would dry up quicker than any
   other plant.
¹³ Such is the destiny of all who forget God;
the hope of the godless will perish.

¹⁴ His source of confidence is fragile;
what he trusts in is a spider's web.
¹⁵ He leans on his web, but it doesn't
   stand firm.
He grabs it, but it does not hold up.
¹⁶ He is a well-watered plant in the sunshine;
his shoots spread out over his garden.
¹⁷ His roots are intertwined around a pile
   of rocks.
He looks for a home among the stones.
¹⁸ If he is uprooted from his place,
it will deny knowing him, saying, "I never
   saw you."
¹⁹ Surely this is the joy of his way of life;
yet others will sprout from the dust.
²⁰ Look, God does not reject a person
   of integrity,
and he will not support evildoers.

²¹ He will yet fill your mouth with laughter
and your lips with a shout of joy.
²² Your enemies will be clothed with shame;
the tent of the wicked will no longer exist.

JOB 9

JOB'S REPLY TO BILDAD

¹ Then Job answered:

² Yes, I know what you've said is true,
but how can a person be justified
   before God?
³ If one wanted to take him to court,
he could not answer God once in a
   thousand times.
⁴ God is wise and all-powerful.
Who has opposed him and come
   out unharmed?

⁵ He removes mountains without their knowledge,
overturning them in his anger.
⁶ He shakes the earth from its place
so that its pillars tremble.
⁷ He commands the sun not to shine
and seals off the stars.
⁸ He alone stretches out the heavens
and treads on the waves of the sea.
⁹ He makes the stars: the Bear, Orion,
the Pleiades, and the constellations of the southern sky.
¹⁰ He does great and unsearchable things,
wonders without number.
¹¹ If he passed by me, I wouldn't see him;
if he went by, I wouldn't recognize him.
¹² If he snatches something, who can stop him?
Who can ask him, "What are you doing?"
¹³ God does not hold back his anger;
Rahab's assistants cringe in fear beneath him!
¹⁴ How then can I answer him
or choose my arguments against him?
¹⁵ Even if I were in the right, I could not answer.
I could only beg my Judge for mercy.
¹⁶ If I summoned him and he answered me,
I do not believe he would pay attention to what I said.
¹⁷ He batters me with a whirlwind
and multiplies my wounds without cause.
¹⁸ He doesn't let me catch my breath
but fills me with bitter experiences.
¹⁹ If it is a matter of strength, look, he is the powerful one!
If it is a matter of justice, who can summon him?
²⁰ Even if I were in the right, my own mouth would condemn me;
if I were blameless, my mouth would declare me guilty.
²¹ Though I am blameless,
I no longer care about myself;
I renounce my life.
²² It is all the same. Therefore I say,
"He destroys both the blameless and the wicked."
²³ When catastrophe brings sudden death,
he mocks the despair of the innocent.
²⁴ The earth is handed over to the wicked;
he blindfolds its judges.
If it isn't he, then who is it?

²⁵ My days fly by faster than a runner;
they flee without seeing any good.
²⁶ They sweep by like boats made of papyrus,
like an eagle swooping down on its prey.
²⁷ If I said, "I will forget my complaint,
change my expression, and smile,"
²⁸ I would still live in terror of all my pains.
I know you will not acquit me.
²⁹ Since I will be found guilty,
why should I struggle in vain?
³⁰ If I wash myself with snow,
and cleanse my hands with lye,
³¹ then you dip me in a pit of mud,
and my own clothes despise me!

³² For he is not a man like me, that I can answer him,
that we can take each other to court.
³³ There is no mediator between us,
to lay his hand on both of us.
³⁴ Let him take his rod away from me
so his terror will no longer frighten me.
³⁵ Then I would speak and not fear him.
But that is not the case; I am on my own.

JOB 10

¹ I am disgusted with my life.
I will give vent to my complaint
and speak in the bitterness of my soul.
² I will say to God,
"Do not declare me guilty!
Let me know why you prosecute me.
³ Is it good for you to oppress,
to reject the work of your hands,
and favor the plans of the wicked?
⁴ Do you have eyes of flesh,
or do you see as a human sees?
⁵ Are your days like those of a human,
or your years like those of a man,
⁶ that you look for my iniquity
and search for my sin,

[7] even though you know that I am not wicked
and that there is no one who can rescue from your power?
[8] "Your hands shaped me and formed me.
Will you now turn and destroy me?
[9] Please remember that you formed me like clay.
Will you now return me to dust?
[10] Did you not pour me out like milk
and curdle me like cheese?
[11] You clothed me with skin and flesh,
and wove me together with bones and tendons.
[12] You gave me life and faithful love,
and your care has guarded my life.

[13] "Yet you concealed these thoughts in your heart;
I know that this was your hidden plan:
[14] if I sin, you would notice,
and would not acquit me of my iniquity.
[15] If I am wicked, woe to me!
And even if I am righteous, I cannot lift up my head.
I am filled with shame
and have drunk deeply of my affliction.
[16] If I am proud, you hunt me like a lion
and again display your miraculous power against me.
[17] You produce new witnesses against me
and multiply your anger toward me.
Hardships assault me, wave after wave.

[18] "Why did you bring me out of the womb?
I should have died and never been seen.
[19] I wish I had never existed
but had been carried from the womb to the grave.
[20] Are my days not few? Stop it!
Leave me alone, so that I can smile a little
[21] before I go to a land of darkness and gloom,
never to return.
[22] It is a land of blackness like the deepest darkness,
gloomy and chaotic,
where even the light is like the darkness."

NAHUM 1:3

The Lord is slow to anger but great in power;
the Lord will never leave the guilty unpunished.
His path is in the whirlwind and storm,
and clouds are the dust beneath his feet.

ROMANS 3:23-26

[23] For all have sinned and fall short of the glory of God. [24] They are justified freely by his grace through the redemption that is in Christ Jesus. [25] God presented him as an atoning sacrifice in his blood, received through faith, to demonstrate his righteousness, because in his restraint God passed over the sins previously committed. [26] God presented him to demonstrate his righteousness at the present time, so that he would be righteous and declare righteous the one who has faith in Jesus.

NOTES

Day 6

GRACE DAY

Each Saturday, we will read a section from God's response to Job in chapter 38.

Use this day to pray, rest, and reflect on this week's reading.

"Where were you when I established the earth? Tell me, if you have understanding. Who fixed its dimensions? Certainly you know! Who stretched a measuring

JOB 38:4–7

line across it? What supports its foundations? Or who laid its cornerstone while the morning stars sang together and all the sons of God shouted for joy?"

Day 7

Weekly

Scripture is God-breathed and true. When we memorize it,
we carry the gospel with us wherever we go.

This week we will memorize Job's initial response to his suffering.

Find the corresponding memory card in the back of this book.

/   /
DATE

Truth

Naked I came from my mother's womb,
and naked I will leave this life.
The Lord gives, and the Lord takes away.
Blessed be the name of the Lord.

JOB 1:21

Day 8

ZOPHAR'S FIRST SPEECH AND JOB'S REPLY

JOB 11–12, PROVERBS 4:18, 1 PETER 2:21–25

JOB 11

ZOPHAR SPEAKS

¹ Then Zophar the Naamathite replied:

² Should this abundance of words
    go unanswered
and such a talker be acquitted?
³ Should your babbling put others
    to silence,
so that you can keep on ridiculing
with no one to humiliate you?
⁴ You have said, "My teaching is sound,
and I am pure in your sight."
⁵ But if only God would speak
and open his lips against you!
⁶ He would show you the secrets of wisdom,
for true wisdom has two sides.
Know then that God has chosen to overlook
    some of your iniquity.

⁷ Can you fathom the depths of God
or discover the limits of the Almighty?
⁸ They are higher than the heavens—what
    can you do?
They are deeper than Sheol—what can
    you know?
⁹ Their measure is longer than the earth
and wider than the sea.

¹⁰ If he passes by and throws someone
    in prison
or convenes a court, who can stop him?
¹¹ Surely he knows which people are
    worthless.
If he sees iniquity, will he not take note
    of it?
¹² But a stupid person will gain understanding
as soon as a wild donkey is born a human!

¹³ As for you, if you redirect your heart
and spread out your hands to him
    in prayer—
¹⁴ if there is iniquity in your hand, remove it,
and don't allow injustice to dwell in
    your tents—
¹⁵ then you will hold your head high, free
    from fault.
You will be firmly established and unafraid.
¹⁶ For you will forget your suffering,
recalling it only as water that has flowed by.
¹⁷ Your life will be brighter than noonday;
its darkness will be like the morning.
¹⁸ You will be confident, because there
    is hope.
You will look carefully about and lie down
    in safety.

¹⁹ You will lie down with no one to
    frighten you,
and many will seek your favor.
²⁰ But the sight of the wicked will fail.
Their way of escape will be cut off,
and their only hope is their last breath.

JOB 12

JOB'S REPLY TO ZOPHAR

¹ Then Job answered:

² No doubt you are the people,
and wisdom will die with you!
³ But I also have a mind like you;
I am not inferior to you.
Who doesn't know the things you are
    talking about?

⁴ I am a laughingstock to my friends,
by calling on God, who answers me.
The righteous and upright man is a
    laughingstock.

⁵ The one who is at ease holds calamity in contempt
and thinks it is prepared for those whose feet are slipping.
⁶ The tents of robbers are safe,
and those who trouble God are secure;
God holds them in his hands.

⁷ But ask the animals, and they will instruct you;
ask the birds of the sky, and they will tell you.
⁸ Or speak to the earth, and it will instruct you;
let the fish of the sea inform you.
⁹ Which of all these does not know
that the hand of the LORD has done this?
¹⁰ The life of every living thing is in his hand,
as well as the breath of all mankind.
¹¹ Doesn't the ear test words
as the palate tastes food?
¹² Wisdom is found with the elderly,
and understanding comes with long life.

¹³ Wisdom and strength belong to God;
counsel and understanding are his.
¹⁴ Whatever he tears down cannot be rebuilt;
whoever he imprisons cannot be released.
¹⁵ When he withholds water, everything dries up,
and when he releases it, it destroys the land.
¹⁶ True wisdom and power belong to him.
The deceived and the deceiver are his.
¹⁷ He leads counselors away barefoot
and makes judges go mad.
¹⁸ He releases the bonds put on by kings
and fastens a belt around their waists.
¹⁹ He leads priests away barefoot
and overthrows established leaders.
²⁰ He deprives trusted advisers of speech
and takes away the elders' good judgment.
²¹ He pours out contempt on nobles
and disarms the strong.
²² He reveals mysteries from the darkness
and brings the deepest darkness into the light.
²³ He makes nations great, then destroys them;
he enlarges nations, then leads them away.

²⁴ He deprives the world's leaders of reason,
   and makes them wander in a
      trackless wasteland.
²⁵ They grope around in darkness
      without light;
   he makes them stagger like a drunkard.

PROVERBS 4:18

The path of the righteous is like the light of dawn,

shining brighter and brighter until midday.

1 PETER 2:21-25

²¹ For you were called to this, because Christ also suffered for you, leaving you an example, that you should follow in his steps. ²² He did not commit sin, and no deceit was found in his mouth; ²³ when he was insulted, he did not insult in return; when he suffered, he did not threaten but entrusted himself to the one who judges justly. ²⁴ He himself bore our sins in his body on the tree; so that, having died to sins, we might live for righteousness. By his wounds you have been healed. ²⁵ For you were like sheep going astray, but you have now returned to the Shepherd and Overseer of your souls.

NOTES

God holds everything in his hands, birds in the sky, everything on land or in water, every living thing and the breath of mankind.

Wisdom & strength belong to God.

[1 Peter 2:21-25] - Similarities to Job's situation.
- Man of complete integrity
- Fears God.
- Trusts God, does not curse the Lord
- Does not talk back or insult his friends.

Job's Counselors

The book of Job is built around interactions between the key figures in the story. The chart below includes descriptions of each figure as well as summaries of their interactions with Job.

Eliphaz

One of Job's friends. Believed Job's suffering must be the result of some sin Job had committed. Urged Job to seek the Lord's favor. Along with Bildad and Zophar, presented in Scripture as a liar and a worthless healer.

EXPLANATION OF JOB'S PLIGHT	ADVICE	JOB'S RESPONSE
In my experience, those who plow injustice and those who sow trouble reap the same. 4:8	…do not reject the discipline of the Almighty. 5:17	I give up! I will not live forever. Leave me alone, for my days are a breath. 7:16
A wicked person writhes in pain all his days… 15:20	Your own mouth condemns you, not I; your own lips testify against you. 15:6	Even now my witness is in heaven, and my advocate is in the heights! 16:19
Isn't your wickedness abundant and aren't your iniquities endless? 22:5	Come to terms with God and be at peace; in this way good will come to you. Receive instruction from his mouth, and place his sayings in your heart. If you return to the Almighty, you will be renewed. 22:21–23	If only I knew how to find him, so that I could go to his throne. I would plead my case before him and fill my mouth with arguments. 23:3–4

Job's Wife

Suffered greatly alongside her husband. Responded to Job's suffering by advising him to curse God and die.

ADVICE	JOB'S RESPONSE
Curse God and die!	Should we accept only good from God and not adversity?
2:9	2:10

Bildad

One of Job's friends. Like Eliphaz, believed Job's suffering was the result of Job's sin. Urged Job to repent and cast himself upon the mercy of God. Suggested Job's children were at fault for their own deaths. Along with Eliphaz and Zophar, presented in Scripture as a liar and a worthless healer.

EXPLANATION OF JOB'S PLIGHT	ADVICE	JOB'S RESPONSE
Does God pervert justice? Does the Almighty pervert what is right?	But if you earnestly seek God and ask the Almighty for mercy, if you are pure and upright, then he will move even now on your behalf and restore the home where your righteousness dwells.	I will say to God, "Do not declare me guilty! Let me know why you prosecute me."
8:3	8:5–6	10:2
Yes, the light of the wicked is extinguished; the flame of his fire does not glow.	How long until you stop talking? Show some sense, and then we can talk.	You have humiliated me ten times now, and you mistreat me without shame.…Have mercy on me, my friends, have mercy, for God's hand has struck me.
18:5	18:2	19:3, 21

	EXPLANATION OF JOB'S PLIGHT	JOB'S RESPONSE
	How can a human be justified before God?	I will never affirm that you are right. I will maintain my integrity until I die.
	25:4	27:5

Zophar

One of Job's friends. Echoed the sentiments of Eliphaz and Bildad. Believed Job's sin must be so great that he likely deserved an even greater punishment than the one he appeared to have received. Along with Eliphaz and Bildad, presented in Scripture as a liar and worthless healer.

EXPLANATION OF JOB'S PLIGHT	ADVICE	JOB'S RESPONSE
If he sees iniquity, will he not take note of it?	As for you, if you redirect your heart and spread out your hands to him in prayer—if there is iniquity in your hand, remove it, and don't allow injustice to dwell in your tents.	I prefer to speak to the Almighty and argue my case before God. You use lies like plaster; you are all worthless healers.
11:11	11:13–14	13:3–4

	EXPLANATION OF JOB'S PLIGHT	JOB'S RESPONSE
	Don't you know that ever since antiquity, from the time a human was placed on earth, the joy of the wicked has been brief and the happiness of the godless has lasted only a moment?	Why do the wicked continue to live, growing old and becoming powerful?
	20:4–5	21:7

Elihu

Fourth friend, introduced at the end of the book. Angry with Job's other friends for not being able to convince Job of his apparent sin. Angry at Job for seeming to lay the blame for his suffering with God. Rebuked Job for being stubborn about admitting sin.

EXPLANATION OF JOB'S PLIGHT	ADVICE
But I tell you that you are wrong in this matter, since God is greater than man. Why do you take him to court for not answering anything a person asks?	If they listen and serve him, they will end their days in prosperity and their years in happiness. But if they do not listen, they will cross the rivear of death and die without knowledge. Those who have a godless heart harbor anger; even when God binds them, they do not cry for help.
33:12–13	36:11–13

The Lord

The Creator of all and the ruler of heaven and earth.

EXPLANATION OF JOB'S PLIGHT

"Who is this who obscures my counsel with ignorant words?"

———————

38:2

ADVICE

"Get ready to answer me like a man; when I question you, you will inform me."

———————

38:3

JOB'S RESPONSE

Therefore, I reject my words and am sorry for them; I am dust and ashes.

———————

42:6

Day 9

JOB CHALLENGES THE ADVICE OF HIS FRIENDS

JOB 13–14, PSALM 71:19–21, JOHN 5:24–25

JOB 13

¹ Look, my eyes have seen all this;
my ears have heard and understood it.
² Everything you know, I also know;
I am not inferior to you.
³ Yet I prefer to speak to the Almighty
and argue my case before God.
⁴ You use lies like plaster;
you are all worthless healers.
⁵ If only you would shut up
and let that be your wisdom!

⁶ Hear now my argument,
and listen to my defense.
⁷ Would you testify unjustly on God's behalf
or speak deceitfully for him?
⁸ Would you show partiality to him
or argue the case in his defense?
⁹ Would it go well if he examined you?
Could you deceive him as you would deceive a man?
¹⁰ Surely he would rebuke you
if you secretly showed partiality.
¹¹ Would God's majesty not terrify you?
Would his dread not fall on you?
¹² Your memorable sayings are proverbs of ash;
your defenses are made of clay.

¹³ Be quiet, and I will speak.
Let whatever comes happen to me.
¹⁴ I will put myself at risk
and take my life in my own hands.
¹⁵ Even if he kills me, I will hope in him.
I will still defend my ways before him.
¹⁶ Yes, this will result in my deliverance,
for no godless person can appear before him.
¹⁷ Pay close attention to my words;
let my declaration ring in your ears.
¹⁸ Now then, I have prepared my case;
I know that I am right.
¹⁹ Can anyone indict me?
If so, I will be silent and die.

²⁰ Only grant these two things to me, God,
so that I will not have to hide from
    your presence:
²¹ remove your hand from me,
and do not let your terror frighten me.
²² Then call, and I will answer,
or I will speak, and you can respond to me.
²³ How many iniquities and sins have
    I committed?
Reveal to me my transgression and sin.
²⁴ Why do you hide your face
and consider me your enemy?
²⁵ Will you frighten a wind-driven leaf?
Will you chase after dry straw?
²⁶ For you record bitter accusations against me
and make me inherit the iniquities of my youth.
²⁷ You put my feet in the stocks
and stand watch over all my paths,
setting a limit for the soles of my feet.

²⁸ A person wears out like something rotten,
like a moth-eaten garment.

JOB 14

¹ Anyone born of woman
is short of days and full of trouble.
² He blossoms like a flower, then withers;
he flees like a shadow and does not last.
³ Do you really take notice of one like this?
Will you bring me into judgment against you?
⁴ Who can produce something pure from what
    is impure?
No one!
⁵ Since a person's days are determined
and the number of his months depends on you,
and since you have set limits he cannot pass,
⁶ look away from him and let him rest
so that he can enjoy his day like a hired worker.

⁷ There is hope for a tree:
If it is cut down, it will sprout again,
and its shoots will not die.
⁸ If its roots grow old in the ground
and its stump starts to die in the soil,
⁹ the scent of water makes it thrive
and produce twigs like a sapling.
¹⁰ But a person dies and fades away;
he breathes his last—where is he?
¹¹ As water disappears from a lake
and a river becomes parched and dry,
¹² so people lie down never to rise again.
They will not wake up until the heavens are
    no more;
they will not stir from their sleep.

¹³ If only you would hide me in Sheol
and conceal me until your anger passes.
If only you would appoint a time for me
and then remember me.
¹⁴ When a person dies, will he come back
    to life?
If so, I would wait all the days of my struggle
until my relief comes.
¹⁵ You would call, and I would answer you.
You would long for the work of your hands.
¹⁶ For then you would count my steps
but would not take note of my sin.
¹⁷ My rebellion would be sealed up in a bag,
and you would cover over my iniquity.

¹⁸ But as a mountain collapses and crumbles
and a rock is dislodged from its place,
¹⁹ as water wears away stones
and torrents wash away the soil from the land,
so you destroy a man's hope.
²⁰ You completely overpower him, and he
    passes on;
you change his appearance and send him away.
²¹ If his sons receive honor, he does not know it;
if they become insignificant, he is unaware of it.
²² He feels only the pain of his own body
and mourns only for himself.

PSALM 71:19-21

[19] Your righteousness reaches the heights, God,
you who have done great things;
God, who is like you?

[20] You caused me to experience many troubles and misfortunes, but you will revive me again. You will bring me up again, even from the depths of the earth.

[21] You will increase my honor
and comfort me once again.

JOHN 5:24-25

LIFE AND JUDGMENT

[24] "Truly I tell you, anyone who hears my word and believes him who sent me has eternal life and will not come under judgment but has passed from death to life.

[25] "Truly I tell you, an hour is coming, and is now here, when the dead will hear the voice of the Son of God, and those who hear will live."

NOTES

Day 10

ELIPHAZ'S SECOND SPEECH AND JOB'S REPLY

JOB 15–17, ROMANS 12:9–15, JAMES 5:8–11

JOB 15

SECOND SERIES OF SPEECHES

ELIPHAZ SPEAKS

¹ Then Eliphaz the Temanite replied:

² Does a wise man answer with
   empty counsel
or fill himself with the hot east wind?
³ Should he argue with useless talk
or with words that serve no good purpose?
⁴ But you even undermine the fear of God
and hinder meditation before him.
⁵ Your iniquity teaches you what to say,
and you choose the language of the crafty.
⁶ Your own mouth condemns you, not I;
your own lips testify against you.

⁷ Were you the first human ever born,
or were you brought forth before the hills?
⁸ Do you listen in on the council of God,
or have a monopoly on wisdom?
⁹ What do you know that we don't?
What do you understand that is not clear
   to us?
¹⁰ Both the gray-haired and the elderly are
   with us—
older than your father.
¹¹ Are God's consolations not enough
   for you,
even the words that deal gently with you?
¹² Why has your heart misled you,
and why do your eyes flash
¹³ as you turn your anger against God
and allow such words to leave your mouth?

¹⁴ What is a mere human, that he should
   be pure,
or one born of a woman, that he should
   be righteous?
¹⁵ If God puts no trust in his holy ones
and the heavens are not pure in his sight,
¹⁶ how much less one who is revolting
   and corrupt,
who drinks injustice like water?

¹⁷ Listen to me and I will inform you.
I will describe what I have seen,
¹⁸ what the wise have declared and
   not concealed,
that came from their ancestors,
¹⁹ to whom alone the land was given
when no foreigner passed among them.
²⁰ A wicked person writhes in pain all
   his days,
throughout the number of years reserved
   for the ruthless.
²¹ Dreadful sounds fill his ears;
when he is at peace, a robber attacks him.
²² He doesn't believe he will return
   from darkness;
he is destined for the sword.
²³ He wanders about for food, asking,
   "Where is it?"
He knows the day of darkness is at hand.
²⁴ Trouble and distress terrify him,
overwhelming him like a king prepared
   for battle.
²⁵ For he has stretched out his hand
   against God
and has arrogantly opposed the Almighty.
²⁶ He rushes headlong at him
with his thick, studded shields.
²⁷ Though his face is covered with fat
and his waistline bulges with it,
²⁸ he will dwell in ruined cities,
in abandoned houses destined to become
   piles of rubble.
²⁹ He will no longer be rich; his wealth will
   not endure.

His possessions will not increase in the land.
³⁰ He will not escape from the darkness;
flames will wither his shoots,
and by the breath of God's mouth, he will depart.
³¹ Let him not put trust in worthless things, being led astray,
for what he gets in exchange will prove worthless.
³² It will be accomplished before his time,
and his branch will not flourish.
³³ He will be like a vine that drops its unripe grapes
and like an olive tree that sheds its blossoms.
³⁴ For the company of the godless will have no children,
and fire will consume the tents of those who offer bribes.
³⁵ They conceive trouble and give birth to evil;
their womb prepares deception.

JOB 16

JOB'S REPLY TO ELIPHAZ

¹ Then Job answered:

² I have heard many things like these.
You are all miserable comforters.
³ Is there no end to your empty words?
What provokes you that you continue testifying?
⁴ If you were in my place I could also talk like you.
I could string words together against you
and shake my head at you.
⁵ Instead, I would encourage you with my mouth,
and the consolation from my lips would bring relief.

⁶ If I speak, my suffering is not relieved,
and if I hold back, does any of it leave me?
⁷ Surely he has now exhausted me.
You have devastated my entire family.
⁸ You have shriveled me up—it has become a witness;
my frailty rises up against me and testifies to my face.
⁹ His anger tears at me, and he harasses me.
He gnashes his teeth at me.
My enemy pierces me with his eyes.
¹⁰ They open their mouths against me
and strike my cheeks with contempt;

they join themselves together against me.
¹¹ God hands me over to the unjust;
he throws me to the wicked.
¹² I was at ease, but he shattered me;
he seized me by the scruff of the neck
and smashed me to pieces.
He set me up as his target;
¹³ his archers surround me.
He pierces my kidneys without mercy
and pours my bile on the ground.
¹⁴ He breaks through my defenses again and again;
he charges at me like a warrior.

¹⁵ I have sewn sackcloth over my skin;
I have buried my strength in the dust.
¹⁶ My face has grown red with weeping,
and darkness covers my eyes,
¹⁷ although my hands are free from violence
and my prayer is pure.
¹⁸ Earth, do not cover my blood;
may my cry for help find no resting place.
¹⁹ Even now my witness is in heaven,
and my advocate is in the heights!
²⁰ My friends scoff at me
as I weep before God.
²¹ I wish that someone might argue for a man with God
just as anyone would for a friend.
²² For only a few years will pass
before I go the way of no return.

JOB 17

¹ My spirit is broken.
My days are extinguished.
A graveyard awaits me.
² Surely mockers surround me,
and my eyes must gaze at their rebellion.

³ Accept my pledge! Put up security for me.
Who else will be my sponsor?

⁴ You have closed their minds to understanding,
therefore you will not honor them.
⁵ If a man denounces his friends for a price,
the eyes of his children will fail.
⁶ He has made me an object of scorn to the people;
I have become a man people spit at.
⁷ My eyes have grown dim from grief,
and my whole body has become but a shadow.
⁸ The upright are appalled at this,
and the innocent are roused against the godless.
⁹ Yet the righteous person will hold to his way,
and the one whose hands are clean will grow stronger.
¹⁰ But come back and try again, all of you.
I will not find a wise man among you.

¹¹ My days have slipped by;
my plans have been ruined,
even the things dear to my heart.
¹² They turned night into day
and made light seem near in the face of darkness.
¹³ If I await Sheol as my home,
spread out my bed in darkness,
¹⁴ and say to corruption, "You are my father,"
and to the maggot, "My mother" or "My sister,"
¹⁵ where then is my hope?
Who can see any hope for me?
¹⁶ Will it go down to the gates of Sheol,
or will we descend together to the dust?

ROMANS 12:9-15

CHRISTIAN ETHICS

⁹ Let love be without hypocrisy. Detest evil; cling to what is good. ¹⁰ Love one another deeply as brothers and sisters. Outdo one another in showing honor. ¹¹ Do not lack diligence in zeal; be fervent in the Spirit; serve the Lord. ¹² Rejoice in hope; be patient in affliction; be persistent in prayer. ¹³ Share with the saints in their needs; pursue hospitality. ¹⁴ Bless those who persecute you; bless and do not curse.

¹⁵ Rejoice with those who rejoice; weep with those who weep.

⁸ You also must be patient. Strengthen your hearts, because the Lord's coming is near.

⁹ Brothers and sisters, do not complain about one another, so that you will not be judged. Look, the judge stands at the door!

¹⁰ Brothers and sisters, take the prophets who spoke in the Lord's name as an example of suffering and patience. ¹¹ See, we count as blessed those who have endured. You have heard of Job's endurance and have seen the outcome that the Lord brought about—the Lord is compassionate and merciful.

NOTES

Day 11

BILDAD'S SECOND SPEECH AND JOB'S REPLY

JOB 18–19, ISAIAH 50:7–10, JOHN 3:17–18

JOB 18

BILDAD SPEAKS

¹ Then Bildad the Shuhite replied:

² How long until you stop talking?
Show some sense, and then we can talk.
³ Why are we regarded as cattle,
as stupid in your sight?
⁴ You who tear yourself in anger—
should the earth be abandoned on your account,
or a rock be removed from its place?

⁵ Yes, the light of the wicked is extinguished;
the flame of his fire does not glow.
⁶ The light in his tent grows dark,
and the lamp beside him is put out.

⁷ His powerful stride is shortened,
and his own schemes trip him up.
⁸ For his own feet lead him into a net,
and he strays into its mesh.
⁹ A trap catches him by the heel;
a noose seizes him.
¹⁰ A rope lies hidden for him on the ground,
and a snare waits for him along the path.
¹¹ Terrors frighten him on every side
and harass him at every step.
¹² His strength is depleted;
disaster lies ready for him to stumble.

¹³ Parts of his skin are eaten away;
death's firstborn consumes his limbs.
¹⁴ He is ripped from the security of his tent
and marched away to the king of terrors.
¹⁵ Nothing he owned remains in his tent.
Burning sulfur is scattered over his home.
¹⁶ His roots below dry up,
and his branches above wither away.
¹⁷ All memory of him perishes from the earth;
he has no name anywhere.

¹⁸ He is driven from light to darkness
and chased from the inhabited world.
¹⁹ He has no children or descendants among his people,
no survivor where he used to live.
²⁰ Those in the west are appalled at his fate,
while those in the east tremble in horror.

²¹ Indeed, such is the dwelling of the unjust man,
and this is the place of the one who does not know God.

JOB 19

JOB'S REPLY TO BILDAD

¹ Then Job answered:

² How long will you torment me
and crush me with words?
³ You have humiliated me ten times now,
and you mistreat me without shame.
⁴ Even if it is true that I have sinned,
my mistake concerns only me.
⁵ If you really want to appear superior to me
and would use my disgrace as evidence against me,
⁶ then understand that it is God who has wronged me
and caught me in his net.
⁷ I cry out: "Violence!" but get no response;
I call for help, but there is no justice.
⁸ He has blocked my way so that I cannot pass through;
he has veiled my paths with darkness.
⁹ He has stripped me of my honor
and removed the crown from my head.
¹⁰ He tears me down on every side so that I am ruined.
He uproots my hope like a tree.
¹¹ His anger burns against me,
and he regards me as one of his enemies.
¹² His troops advance together;
they construct a ramp against me
and camp around my tent.
¹³ He has removed my brothers from me;
my acquaintances have abandoned me.

¹⁴ My relatives stop coming by,
and my close friends have forgotten me.
¹⁵ My house guests and female servants regard me as a stranger;
I am a foreigner in their sight.
¹⁶ I call for my servant, but he does not answer,
even if I beg him with my own mouth.
¹⁷ My breath is offensive to my wife,
and my own family finds me repulsive.
¹⁸ Even young boys scorn me.
When I stand up, they mock me.
¹⁹ All of my best friends despise me.
and those I love have turned against me.
²⁰ My skin and my flesh cling to my bones;
I have escaped with only the skin of my teeth.
²¹ Have mercy on me, my friends, have mercy,
for God's hand has struck me.
²² Why do you persecute me as God does?
Will you never get enough of my flesh?

²³ I wish that my words were written down,
that they were recorded on a scroll
²⁴ or were inscribed in stone forever
by an iron stylus and lead!
²⁵ But I know that my Redeemer lives,
and at the end he will stand on the dust.
²⁶ Even after my skin has been destroyed,
yet I will see God in my flesh.
²⁷ I will see him myself;
my eyes will look at him, and not as a stranger.
My heart longs within me.

²⁸ If you say, "How will we pursue him,
since the root of the problem lies with him?"
²⁹ then be afraid of the sword,
because wrath brings punishment by the sword,
so that you may know there is a judgment.

ISAIAH 50:7-10

⁷ The Lord God will help me;
therefore I have not been humiliated;
therefore I have set my face like flint,
and I know I will not be put to shame.
⁸ The one who vindicates me is near;
who will contend with me?
Let us confront each other.
Who has a case against me?
Let him come near me!

⁹ In truth, the Lord God will help me;
who will condemn me?
Indeed, all of them will wear out like a garment;
a moth will devour them.
¹⁰ Who among you fears the Lord
and listens to his servant?
Who among you walks in darkness,
and has no light?

Let him trust in the name of the Lord;

let him lean on his God.

JOHN 3:17-18

¹⁷ "For God did not send his Son into the world to condemn the world, but to save the world through him. ¹⁸ Anyone who believes in him is not condemned, but anyone who does not believe is already condemned, because he has not believed in the name of the one and only Son of God."

NOTES

Day 12

ZOPHAR'S SECOND SPEECH AND JOB'S REPLY

JOB 20–21, PSALM 37:34–36, 2 PETER 3:9–13

JOB 20

ZOPHAR SPEAKS

¹ Then Zophar the Naamathite replied:

² This is why my unsettling thoughts compel me to answer,
because I am upset!
³ I have heard a rebuke that insults me,
and my understanding makes me reply.

⁴ Don't you know that ever since antiquity,
from the time a human was placed on earth,
⁵ the joy of the wicked has been brief
and the happiness of the godless has lasted only a moment?
⁶ Though his arrogance reaches heaven,
and his head touches the clouds,
⁷ he will vanish forever like his own dung.
Those who know him will ask, "Where is he?"
⁸ He will fly away like a dream and never be found;
he will be chased away like a vision in the night.
⁹ The eye that saw him will see him no more,
and his household will no longer see him.
¹⁰ His children will beg from the poor,
for his own hands must give back his wealth.
¹¹ His frame may be full of youthful vigor,
but it will lie down with him in dust.

¹² Though evil tastes sweet in his mouth
and he conceals it under his tongue,
¹³ though he cherishes it and will not let it go
but keeps it in his mouth,
¹⁴ yet the food in his stomach turns
into cobras' venom inside him.
¹⁵ He swallows wealth but must vomit it up;
God will force it from his stomach.
¹⁶ He will suck the poison of cobras;
a viper's fangs will kill him.
¹⁷ He will not enjoy the streams,
the rivers flowing with honey and curds.
¹⁸ He must return the fruit of his labor without consuming it;
he doesn't enjoy the profits from his trading.
¹⁹ For he oppressed and abandoned the poor;
he seized a house he did not build.

²⁰ Because his appetite is never satisfied,
he does not let anything he desires escape.
²¹ Nothing is left for him to consume;
therefore, his prosperity will not last.
²² At the height of his success distress will come to him;
the full weight of misery will crush him.
²³ When he fills his stomach,
God will send his burning anger against him,
raining it down on him while he is eating.
²⁴ If he flees from an iron weapon,
an arrow from a bronze bow will pierce him.
²⁵ He pulls it out of his back,
the flashing tip out of his liver.
Terrors come over him.
²⁶ Total darkness is reserved for his treasures.
A fire unfanned by human hands will consume him;
it will feed on what is left in his tent.
²⁷ The heavens will expose his iniquity,
and the earth will rise up against him.
²⁸ The possessions in his house will be removed,
flowing away on the day of God's anger.
²⁹ This is the wicked person's lot from God,
the inheritance God ordained for him.

JOB 21

JOB'S REPLY TO ZOPHAR

¹ Then Job answered:

² Pay close attention to my words;
let this be the consolation you offer.
³ Bear with me while I speak;
then after I have spoken, you may continue mocking.

⁴ As for me, is my complaint against a human being?
Then why shouldn't I be impatient?
⁵ Look at me and shudder;
put your hand over your mouth.
⁶ When I think about it, I am terrified
and my body trembles in horror.

⁷ Why do the wicked continue to live,
growing old and becoming powerful?
⁸ Their children are established while they are still alive,
and their descendants, before their eyes.
⁹ Their homes are secure and free of fear;
no rod from God strikes them.
¹⁰ Their bulls breed without fail;
their cows calve and do not miscarry.
¹¹ They let their little ones run around like lambs;
their children skip about,
¹² singing to the tambourine and lyre
and rejoicing at the sound of the flute.
¹³ They spend their days in prosperity
and go down to Sheol in peace.
¹⁴ Yet they say to God, "Leave us alone!
We don't want to know your ways.
¹⁵ Who is the Almighty, that we should serve him,
and what will we gain by pleading with him?"
¹⁶ But their prosperity is not of their own doing.
The counsel of the wicked is far from me!

¹⁷ How often is the lamp of the wicked put out?
Does disaster come on them?
Does he apportion destruction in his anger?
¹⁸ Are they like straw before the wind,
like chaff a storm sweeps away?
¹⁹ God reserves a person's punishment for his children.
Let God repay the person himself, so that he may know it.
²⁰ Let his own eyes see his demise;
let him drink from the Almighty's wrath!
²¹ For what does he care about his family once he is dead,
when the number of his months has run out?

²² Can anyone teach God knowledge,
since he judges the exalted ones?
²³ One person dies in excellent health,
completely secure and at ease.
²⁴ His body is well fed,
and his bones are full of marrow.
²⁵ Yet another person dies with a bitter soul,
having never tasted prosperity.

²⁶ But they both lie in the dust,
and worms cover them.

²⁷ I know your thoughts very well,
the schemes by which you would wrong me.
²⁸ For you say, "Where now is the nobleman's house?"
and "Where are the tents the wicked lived in?"
²⁹ Have you never consulted those who travel the roads?
Don't you accept their reports?
³⁰ Indeed, the evil person is spared from the day of disaster,
rescued from the day of wrath.
³¹ Who would denounce his behavior to his face?
Who would repay him for what he has done?
³² He is carried to the grave,
and someone keeps watch over his tomb.
³³ The dirt on his grave is sweet to him.
Everyone follows behind him,
and those who go before him are without number.

³⁴ So how can you offer me such futile comfort?
Your answers are deceptive.

PSALM 37:34-36

**³⁴ Wait for the Lord and keep his way,
and he will exalt you to inherit the land.
You will watch when the wicked are destroyed.**

³⁵ I have seen a wicked, violent person
well-rooted, like a flourishing native tree.
³⁶ Then I passed by and noticed he was gone;
I searched for him, but he could not be found.

NOTES

Day 13

GRACE DAY

Use this day to pray, rest, and reflect on this week's reading.

"Have you traveled to the sources of the sea or walked in the depths of the oceans? Have the gates of death been revealed to you?

JOB 38:16–18

Have you seen the gates of deep darkness? Have you comprehended the extent of the earth? Tell me, if you know all this."

Day 14

Weekly

Scripture is God-breathed and true. When we memorize it, we carry the gospel with us wherever we go.

Over the remainder of this study, we will memorize Job 19:25–27. This week we will memorize the key verse for this plan, Job 19:25.

Find the corresponding memory card in the back of this book.

/   /
DATE

Truth

But I know that my Redeemer lives,
and at the end he will stand on the dust.

JOB 19:25

Day 15

ELIPHAZ'S THIRD SPEECH AND JOB'S REPLY

JOB 22–24, ROMANS 8:1–2, GALATIANS 6:7–10

JOB 22

THIRD SERIES OF SPEECHES

ELIPHAZ SPEAKS

¹ Then Eliphaz the Temanite replied:

² Can a man be of any use to God?
Can even a wise man be of use to him?
³ Does it delight the Almighty if you are righteous?
Does he profit if you perfect your behavior?

⁴ Does he correct you and take you to court
because of your piety?
⁵ Isn't your wickedness abundant
and aren't your iniquities endless?
⁶ For you took collateral from your brothers without cause,
stripping off their clothes and leaving them naked.
⁷ You gave no water to the thirsty
and withheld food from the famished,
⁸ while the land belonged to a powerful man
and an influential man lived on it.
⁹ You sent widows away empty-handed,
and the strength of the fatherless was crushed.
¹⁰ Therefore snares surround you,
and sudden dread terrifies you,
¹¹ or darkness, so you cannot see,
and a flood of water covers you.

¹² Isn't God as high as the heavens?
And look at the highest stars—how lofty they are!
¹³ Yet you say, "What does God know?
Can he judge through total darkness?
¹⁴ Clouds veil him so that he cannot see,
as he walks on the circle of the sky."
¹⁵ Will you continue on the ancient path
that wicked men have walked?
¹⁶ They were snatched away before their time,
and their foundations were washed away by a river.
¹⁷ They were the ones who said to God, "Leave us alone!"
and "What can the Almighty do to us?"
¹⁸ But it was he who filled their houses with good things.
The counsel of the wicked is far from me!

[19] The righteous see this and rejoice;
the innocent mock them, saying,
[20] "Surely our opponents are destroyed,
and fire has consumed what they left behind."

[21] Come to terms with God and be at peace;
in this way good will come to you.
[22] Receive instruction from his mouth,
and place his sayings in your heart.
[23] If you return to the Almighty, you will be renewed.
If you banish injustice from your tent
[24] and consign your gold to the dust,
the gold of Ophir to the stones in the wadis,
[25] the Almighty will be your gold
and your finest silver.
[26] Then you will delight in the Almighty
and lift up your face to God.
[27] You will pray to him, and he will hear you,
and you will fulfill your vows.
[28] When you make a decision, it will be carried out,
and light will shine on your ways.
[29] When others are humiliated and you say, "Lift them up,"
God will save the humble.
[30] He will even rescue the guilty one,
who will be rescued by the purity of your hands.

JOB 23

JOB'S REPLY TO ELIPHAZ

[1] Then Job answered:

[2] Today also my complaint is bitter.
His hand is heavy despite my groaning.
[3] If only I knew how to find him,
so that I could go to his throne.
[4] I would plead my case before him
and fill my mouth with arguments.
[5] I would learn how he would answer me;
and understand what he would say to me.
[6] Would he prosecute me forcefully?
No, he would certainly pay attention to me.

⁷ Then an upright man could reason with him,
and I would escape from my Judge forever.

⁸ If I go east, he is not there,
and if I go west, I cannot perceive him.
⁹ When he is at work to the north, I cannot see him;
when he turns south, I cannot find him.
¹⁰ Yet he knows the way I have taken;
when he has tested me, I will emerge as pure gold.
¹¹ My feet have followed in his tracks;
I have kept to his way and not turned aside.
¹² I have not departed from the commands from his lips;
I have treasured the words from his mouth
more than my daily food.

¹³ But he is unchangeable; who can oppose him?
He does what he desires.
¹⁴ He will certainly accomplish what he has decreed for me,
and he has many more things like these in mind.
¹⁵ Therefore I am terrified in his presence;
when I consider this, I am afraid of him.
¹⁶ God has made my heart faint;
the Almighty has terrified me.
¹⁷ Yet I am not destroyed by the darkness,
by the thick darkness that covers my face.

JOB 24

¹ Why does the Almighty not reserve times for judgment?
Why do those who know him never see his days?
² The wicked displace boundary markers.
They steal a flock and provide pasture for it.
³ They drive away the donkeys owned by the fatherless
and take the widow's ox as collateral.
⁴ They push the needy off the road;
the poor of the land are forced into hiding.
⁵ Like wild donkeys in the wilderness,
the poor go out to their task of foraging for food;
the desert provides nourishment for their children.
⁶ They gather their fodder in the field
and glean the vineyards of the wicked.

⁷ Without clothing, they spend the night naked,
having no covering against the cold.
⁸ Drenched by mountain rains,
they huddle against the rocks, shelterless.
⁹ The fatherless infant is snatched from the breast;
the nursing child of the poor is seized as collateral.
¹⁰ Without clothing, they wander about naked.
They carry sheaves but go hungry.
¹¹ They crush olives in their presses;
they tread the winepresses, but go thirsty.
¹² From the city, men groan;
the mortally wounded cry for help,
yet God pays no attention to this crime.

¹³ The wicked are those who rebel against the light.
They do not recognize its ways
or stay on its paths.
¹⁴ The murderer rises at dawn
to kill the poor and needy,
and by night he becomes a thief.
¹⁵ The adulterer's eye watches for twilight,
thinking, "No eye will see me,"
and he covers his face.
¹⁶ In the dark they break into houses;
by day they lock themselves in,
never experiencing the light.
¹⁷ For the morning is like darkness to them.
Surely they are familiar with the terrors of darkness!

¹⁸ They float on the surface of the water.
Their section of the land is cursed,
so that they never go to their vineyards.
¹⁹ As dry ground and heat snatch away the melted snow,
so Sheol steals those who have sinned.
²⁰ The womb forgets them;
worms feed on them;
they are remembered no more.
So injustice is broken like a tree.
²¹ They prey on the childless woman who is unable to conceive,
and do not deal kindly with the widow.
²² Yet God drags away the mighty by his power;
when he rises up, they have no assurance of life.

²³ He gives them a sense of security, so they can rely on it,
but his eyes watch over their ways.
²⁴ They are exalted for a moment, then gone;
they are brought low and shrivel up like everything else.
They wither like heads of grain.

²⁵ If this is not true, then who can prove me a liar
and show that my speech is worthless?

ROMANS 8:1-2

¹ Therefore, there is now no condemnation for those in Christ Jesus, ² because the law of the Spirit of life in Christ Jesus has set you free from the law of sin and death.

GALATIANS 6:7-10

⁷ Don't be deceived: God is not mocked. For whatever a person sows he will also reap, ⁸ because the one who sows to his flesh will reap destruction from the flesh, but the one who sows to the Spirit will reap eternal life from the Spirit. ⁹ Let us not get tired of doing good, for we will reap at the proper time if we don't give up. ¹⁰ Therefore, as we have opportunity, let us work for the good of all, especially for those who belong to the household of faith.

NOTES

Day 16

BILDAD'S THIRD SPEECH AND JOB'S REPLY

JOB 25–27, PSALM 119:9–16, 1 JOHN 1:8–10

JOB 25

BILDAD SPEAKS

¹ Then Bildad the Shuhite replied:

² Dominion and dread belong to him,
the one who establishes harmony in his heights.
³ Can his troops be numbered?
Does his light not shine on everyone?
⁴ How can a human be justified before God?
How can one born of woman be pure?
⁵ If even the moon does not shine
and the stars are not pure in his sight,
⁶ how much less a human, who is a maggot,
a son of man, who is a worm!

JOB 26

JOB'S REPLY TO BILDAD

¹ Then Job answered:

² How you have helped the powerless
and delivered the arm that is weak!
³ How you have counseled the unwise
and abundantly provided insight!
⁴ With whom did you speak these words?
Whose breath came out of your mouth?

⁵ The departed spirits tremble
beneath the waters and all that inhabit them.
⁶ Sheol is naked before God,
and Abaddon has no covering.

⁷ He stretches the northern skies over empty space;
he hangs the earth on nothing.
⁸ He wraps up the water in his clouds,
yet the clouds do not burst beneath its weight.
⁹ He obscures the view of his throne,
spreading his cloud over it.
¹⁰ He laid out the horizon on the surface of the waters
at the boundary between light and darkness.

¹¹ The pillars that hold up the sky tremble,
astounded at his rebuke.
¹² By his power he stirred the sea,
and by his understanding he
    crushed Rahab.

¹³ By his breath the heavens gained
    their beauty;
his hand pierced the fleeing serpent.
¹⁴ These are but the fringes of his ways;
how faint is the word we hear of him!
Who can understand his mighty thunder?

JOB 27

¹ Job continued his discourse, saying:

² As God lives, who has deprived me
    of justice,
and the Almighty who has made me bitter,
³ as long as my breath is still in me
and the breath from God remains in
    my nostrils,
⁴ my lips will not speak unjustly,
and my tongue will not utter deceit.
⁵ I will never affirm that you are right.
I will maintain my integrity until I die.
⁶ I will cling to my righteousness and never
    let it go.
My conscience will not accuse me as long
    as I live!
⁷ May my enemy be like the wicked
and my opponent like the unjust.
⁸ For what hope does the godless person
    have when he is cut off,
when God takes away his life?
⁹ Will God hear his cry
when distress comes on him?

¹⁰ Will he delight in the Almighty?
Will he call on God at all times?
¹¹ I will teach you about God's power.
I will not conceal what the Almighty
    has planned.
¹² All of you have seen this for yourselves,
why do you keep up this empty talk?
¹³ This is a wicked man's lot from God,
the inheritance the ruthless receive from
    the Almighty.
¹⁴ Even if his children increase, they are
destined for the sword;
his descendants will never have
    enough food.
¹⁵ Those who survive him will be buried by
    the plague,
yet their widows will not weep for them.
¹⁶ Though he piles up silver like dust
and heaps up fine clothing like clay—
¹⁷ he may heap it up, but the righteous will
    wear it,
and the innocent will divide up his silver.
¹⁸ The house he built is like a moth's cocoon
or a shelter set up by a watchman.
¹⁹ He lies down wealthy, but will do so
    no more;
when he opens his eyes, it is gone.
²⁰ Terrors overtake him like a flood;
a storm wind sweeps him away at night.
²¹ An east wind picks him up, and he
    is gone;
it carries him away from his place.
²² It blasts at him without mercy,
while he flees desperately from its force.
²³ It claps its hands at him
and scoffs at him from its place.

PSALM 119:9-16

ב BETH

⁹ How can a young man keep his way pure?
By keeping your word.

¹⁰ I have sought you with all my heart; don't let me wander from your commands.

¹¹ I have treasured your word in my heart
so that I may not sin against you.
¹² Lord, may you be blessed;
teach me your statutes.
¹³ With my lips I proclaim
all the judgments from your mouth.
¹⁴ I rejoice in the way revealed by
    your decrees
as much as in all riches.
¹⁵ I will meditate on your precepts
and think about your ways.
¹⁶ I will delight in your statutes;
I will not forget your word.

1 JOHN 1:8-10

⁸ If we say, "We have no sin," we are deceiving ourselves, and the truth is not in us. ⁹ If we confess our sins, he is faithful and righteous to forgive us our sins and to cleanse us from all unrighteousness. ¹⁰ If we say, "We have not sinned," we make him a liar, and his word is not in us.

NOTES

Day 17

WHERE IS WISDOM FOUND?

JOB 28–29, PROVERBS 1:7, 1 CORINTHIANS 1:28–31

JOB 28

A HYMN TO WISDOM

[1] Surely there is a mine for silver
and a place where gold is refined.
[2] Iron is taken from the ground,
and copper is smelted from ore.
[3] A miner puts an end to the darkness;
he probes the deepest recesses
for ore in the gloomy darkness.
[4] He cuts a shaft far from human habitation,
in places unknown to those who walk
    above ground.
Suspended far away from people,
the miners swing back and forth.
[5] Food may come from the earth,
but below the surface the earth is transformed
    as by fire.
[6] Its rocks are a source of lapis lazuli,
containing flecks of gold.
[7] No bird of prey knows that path;
no falcon's eye has seen it.
[8] Proud beasts have never walked on it;
no lion has ever prowled over it.
[9] The miner uses a flint tool
and turns up ore from the root of
    the mountains.
[10] He cuts out channels in the rocks,
and his eyes spot every treasure.
[11] He dams up the streams from flowing
so that he may bring to light what is hidden.
[12] But where can wisdom be found, and where
is understanding located?
[13] No one can know its value,
since it cannot be found in the land of
    the living.
[14] The ocean depths say, "It's not in me,"
while the sea declares, "I don't have it."
[15] Gold cannot be exchanged for it,
and silver cannot be weighed out for its price.
[16] Wisdom cannot be valued in the gold of Ophir,
in precious onyx or lapis lazuli.
[17] Gold and glass do not compare with it,
and articles of fine gold cannot be exchanged
    for it.
[18] Coral and quartz are not worth mentioning.
The price of wisdom is beyond pearls.
[19] Topaz from Cush cannot compare with it,
and it cannot be valued in pure gold.
[20] Where then does wisdom come from, and
where is understanding located?
[21] It is hidden from the eyes of every living thing
and concealed from the birds of the sky.
[22] Abaddon and Death say,
"We have heard news of it with our ears."
[23] But God understands the way to wisdom,
and he knows its location.
[24] For he looks to the ends of the earth
and sees everything under the heavens.
[25] When God fixed the weight of the wind
and distributed the water by measure,
[26] when he established a limit for the rain
and a path for the lightning,
[27] he considered wisdom and evaluated it;
he established it and examined it.
[28] He said to mankind,

> **"The fear of the LORD—that is wisdom. And to turn from evil is understanding."**

JOB 29

JOB'S FINAL CLAIM OF INNOCENCE

[1] Job continued his discourse, saying:

[2] If only I could be as in months gone by,
in the days when God watched over me,
[3] when his lamp shone above my head,

and I walked through darkness by his light!
⁴ I would be as I was in the days of my youth
when God's friendship rested on my tent,
⁵ when the Almighty was still with me
and my children were around me,
⁶ when my feet were bathed in curds
and the rock poured out streams of oil for me!

⁷ When I went out to the city gate
and took my seat in the town square,
⁸ the young men saw me and withdrew,
while older men stood to their feet.
⁹ City officials stopped talking
and covered their mouths with their hands.
¹⁰ The noblemen's voices were hushed,
and their tongues stuck to the roof of their mouths.
¹¹ When they heard me, they blessed me,
and when they saw me, they spoke well of me.
¹² For I rescued the poor who cried out for help,
and the fatherless child who had no one to support him.
¹³ The dying blessed me,
and I made the widow's heart rejoice.
¹⁴ I clothed myself in righteousness,
and it enveloped me;
my just decisions were like a robe and a turban.
¹⁵ I was eyes to the blind
and feet to the lame.
¹⁶ I was a father to the needy,
and I examined the case of the stranger.
¹⁷ I shattered the fangs of the unjust
and snatched the prey from his teeth.

¹⁸ So I thought, "I will die in my own nest
and multiply my days as the sand.
¹⁹ My roots will have access to water,
and the dew will rest on my branches all night.
²⁰ My whole being will be refreshed within me,
and my bow will be renewed in my hand."

²¹ Men listened to me with expectation,
waiting silently for my advice.
²² After a word from me they did not speak again;

my speech settled on them like dew.
²³ They waited for me as for the rain
and opened their mouths as for
   spring showers.
²⁴ If I smiled at them, they couldn't believe it;
they were thrilled at the light of my
   countenance.
²⁵ I directed their course and presided
   as chief.
I lived as a king among his troops,
like one who comforts those who mourn.

PROVERBS 1:7

The fear of the LORD
is the beginning of knowledge;
fools despise wisdom and discipline.

1 CORINTHIANS 1:28-31

²⁸ God has chosen what is insignificant and despised in the world—what is viewed as nothing—to bring to nothing what is viewed as something, ²⁹ so that no one may boast in his presence. ³⁰ It is from him that you are in Christ Jesus,

who became wisdom from God for us—our righteousness, sanctification, and redemption, ³¹ in order that, as it is written: Let the one who boasts, boast in the Lord.

NOTES

Trials of Many Kinds

Jesus told His disciples in John 16:33, "You will have suffering in this world." Not only does Scripture tell us to expect suffering, James 1:2–4 says to "consider it a great joy" when we "experience various trials" because it matures our faith.

While Job's story of suffering is perhaps the most well-known, there are numerous references to human suffering throughout Scripture. Below are some of the most common types of suffering found in the Bible.

Catastrophe

GN 12:10; LK 13:1-4

Suffering brought on by unpredictable and unprovoked natural or man-made disasters like hurricanes, earthquakes, train crashes, tsunamis, building collapses, famine, and plagues.

Collective Suffering

GN 47:13; EX 8:21-23

The pain of belonging to a people who are suffering together, as seen in famine, drought, or war. Also seen in Scripture when God disciplines entire nations.

Discipline

2SM 11-12; PS 51

Suffering designed to lead to correction and repentance.

Intentional Suffering

JNH 3:5; MT 4:1-2

Self-discipline, such as fasting or denial of creature comforts, for the purpose of spiritual growth.

Judgment

GN 4:13-14; 1KG 2:32

Suffering brought about because of disobedience to God or people in positions of power.

Mysterious Suffering

JB 3:20-26; MK 5:25-34

Suffering for reasons that are unknown or not revealed by God.

Natural Consequences

MT 7:26-27; LK 15:11-32

Suffering that results from foolish decisions, ignorance, or decay.

Persecution

EST 3:5-6; AC 7:54-60

Suffering introduced by an enemy, whether spiritual or physical, that is intended to cause harm.

Physical Pain

JB 14:22; MT 4:23-25

Bodily distress or trauma.

Purposeful Suffering

GN 50:20; IS 53:5

Suffering that brings about a greater, often hidden, purpose.

Sympathy

NEH 1:1-11; MT 9:36

Pain experienced in response to another person or group's suffering; hurting when a loved one hurts.

Training

JB 1-2; 2CO 12:1-10

Suffering that is not connected to failure, but is intended to bring about spiritual growth and maturity.

Day 18

JOB SPEAKS ABOUT HIS CONDITION

JOB 30–31, PSALM 42:4, MATTHEW 27:45–46

JOB 30

¹ But now they mock me,
men younger than I am,
whose fathers I would have refused to put
with my sheep dogs.
² What use to me was the strength of their hands?
Their vigor had left them.
³ Emaciated from poverty and hunger,
they gnawed the dry land,
the desolate wasteland by night.
⁴ They plucked mallow among the shrubs,
and the roots of the broom tree were their food.
⁵ They were banished from human society;
people shouted at them as if they were thieves.
⁶ They are living on the slopes of the wadis,
among the rocks and in holes in the ground.
⁷ They bray among the shrubs;
they huddle beneath the thistles.
⁸ Foolish men, without even a name.
They were forced to leave the land.

⁹ Now I am mocked by their songs;
I have become an object of scorn to them.
¹⁰ They despise me and keep their distance from me;
they do not hesitate to spit in my face.
¹¹ Because God has loosened my bowstring and oppressed me,
they have cast off restraint in my presence.
¹² The rabble rise up at my right;
they trap my feet
and construct their siege ramp against me.
¹³ They tear up my path;
they contribute to my destruction,
without anyone to help them.
¹⁴ They advance as through a gaping breach;
they keep rolling in through the ruins.
¹⁵ Terrors are turned loose against me;
they chase my dignity away like the wind,
and my prosperity has passed by like a cloud.

¹⁶ Now my life is poured out before me,
and days of suffering have seized me.

¹⁷ Night pierces my bones,
but my gnawing pains never rest.
¹⁸ My clothing is distorted with great force;
he chokes me by the neck of my garment.
¹⁹ He throws me into the mud,
and I have become like dust and ashes.

²⁰ I cry out to you for help, but you do not answer me;
when I stand up, you merely look at me.
²¹ You have turned against me with cruelty;
you harass me with your strong hand.
²² You lift me up on the wind and make me ride it;
you scatter me in the storm.
²³ Yes, I know that you will lead me to death—
the place appointed for all who live.

²⁴ Yet no one would stretch out his hand
against a ruined person
when he cries out to him for help
because of his distress.
²⁵ Have I not wept for those who have fallen on hard times?
Has my soul not grieved for the needy?
²⁶ But when I hoped for good, evil came;
when I looked for light, darkness came.
²⁷ I am churning within and cannot rest;
days of suffering confront me.
²⁸ I walk about blackened, but not by the sun.
I stood in the assembly and cried out for help.
²⁹ I have become a brother to jackals
and a companion of ostriches.
³⁰ My skin blackens and flakes off,
and my bones burn with fever.
³¹ My lyre is used for mourning
and my flute for the sound of weeping.

JOB 31

¹ I have made a covenant with my eyes.
How then could I look at a young woman?
² For what portion would I have from God above,
or what inheritance from the Almighty on high?

³ Doesn't disaster come to the unjust
and misfortune to evildoers?
⁴ Does he not see my ways
and number all my steps?

⁵ If I have walked in falsehood
or my foot has rushed to deceit,
⁶ let God weigh me on accurate scales,
and he will recognize my integrity.

⁷ If my step has turned from the way,
my heart has followed my eyes,
or impurity has stained my hands,
⁸ let someone else eat what I have sown,
and let my crops be uprooted.

⁹ If my heart has gone astray over a woman
or I have lurked at my neighbor's door,
¹⁰ let my own wife grind grain for another man,
and let other men sleep with her.
¹¹ For that would be a disgrace;
it would be an iniquity deserving punishment.
¹² For it is a fire that consumes down to Abaddon;
it would destroy my entire harvest.

¹³ If I have dismissed the case of my male or female servants
when they made a complaint against me,
¹⁴ what could I do when God stands up to judge?
How should I answer him when he calls me to account?
¹⁵ Did not the one who made me in the womb also make them?
Did not the same God form us both in the womb?

¹⁶ If I have refused the wishes of the poor
or let the widow's eyes go blind,
¹⁷ if I have eaten my few crumbs alone
without letting the fatherless eat any of it—
¹⁸ for from my youth, I raised him as his father,
and since the day I was born I guided the widow—
¹⁹ if I have seen anyone dying for lack of clothing
or a needy person without a cloak,

[20] if he did not bless me
while warming himself with the fleece from my sheep,
[21] if I ever cast my vote against a fatherless child
when I saw that I had support in the city gate,
[22] then let my shoulder blade fall from my back,
and my arm be pulled from its socket.
[23] For disaster from God terrifies me,
and because of his majesty I could not do these things.

[24] If I placed my confidence in gold
or called fine gold my trust,
[25] if I have rejoiced because my wealth is great
or because my own hand has acquired so much,
[26] if I have gazed at the sun when it was shining
or at the moon moving in splendor,
[27] so that my heart was secretly enticed
and I threw them a kiss,
[28] this would also be an iniquity deserving punishment,
for I would have denied God above.

[29] Have I rejoiced over my enemy's distress,
or become excited when trouble came his way?
[30] I have not allowed my mouth to sin
by asking for his life with a curse.
[31] Haven't the members of my household said,
"Who is there who has not had enough to eat at Job's table?"
[32] No stranger had to spend the night on the street,
for I opened my door to the traveler.
[33] Have I covered my transgressions as others do
by hiding my iniquity in my heart
[34] because I greatly feared the crowds
and because the contempt of the clans terrified me,
so I grew silent and would not go outside?

[35] If only I had someone to hear my case!
Here is my signature; let the Almighty answer me.
Let my Opponent compose his indictment.
[36] I would surely carry it on my shoulder
and wear it like a crown.

³⁷ I would give him an account of all
   my steps;
I would approach him like a prince.

³⁸ If my land cries out against me
and its furrows join in weeping,
³⁹ if I have consumed its produce
   without payment
or shown contempt for its tenants,
⁴⁰ then let thorns grow instead of wheat
and stinkweed instead of barley.

The words of Job are concluded.

PSALM 42:4

I remember this as I pour out my heart:
how I walked with many,
leading the festive procession to the house
   of God,
with joyful and thankful shouts.

MATTHEW 27:45-46

THE DEATH OF JESUS

⁴⁵ From noon until three in the afternoon darkness came over the whole land. ⁴⁶ About three in the afternoon Jesus cried out with a loud voice, *"Elí, Elí, lemá sabachtháni?"* that is, "My God, my God, why have you abandoned me?"

NOTES

Day 19

ELIHU SPEAKS TO JOB'S CONDITION

JOB 32–33, PSALM 118:8, MARK 12:28–31

JOB 32

ELIHU'S ANGRY RESPONSE

¹ So these three men quit answering Job, because he was righteous in his own eyes. ² Then Elihu son of Barachel the Buzite from the family of Ram became angry. He was angry at Job because he had justified himself rather than God. ³ He was also angry at Job's three friends because they had failed to refute him and yet had condemned him.

⁴ Now Elihu had waited to speak to Job because they were all older than he. ⁵ But when he saw that the three men could not answer Job, he became angry.

⁶ So Elihu son of Barachel the Buzite replied:

> I am young in years,
> while you are old;
> therefore I was timid and afraid
> to tell you what I know.
> ⁷ I thought that age should speak
> and maturity should teach wisdom.
> ⁸ But it is the spirit in a person—
> the breath from the Almighty—
> that gives anyone understanding.
> ⁹ It is not only the old who are wise
> or the elderly who understand how to judge.
> ¹⁰ Therefore I say, "Listen to me.
> I too will declare what I know."
> ¹¹ Look, I waited for your conclusions;
> I listened to your insights
> as you sought for words.
> ¹² I paid close attention to you.
> Yet no one proved Job wrong;
> not one of you refuted his arguments.
> ¹³ So do not claim, "We have found wisdom;
> let God deal with him, not man."
>
> ¹⁴ But Job has not directed his argument to me,
> and I will not respond to him with your arguments.
> ¹⁵ Job's friends are dismayed and can no longer answer;
> words have left them.
> ¹⁶ Should I continue to wait now that they are silent,

now that they stand there and no longer answer?
¹⁷ I too will answer;
yes, I will tell what I know.
¹⁸ For I am full of words,
and my spirit compels me to speak.
¹⁹ My heart is like unvented wine;
it is about to burst like new wineskins.
²⁰ I must speak so that I can find relief;
I must open my lips and respond.
²¹ I will be partial to no one,
and I will not give anyone an undeserved title.
²² For I do not know how to give such titles;
otherwise, my Maker would remove me in an instant.

JOB 33

ELIHU CONFRONTS JOB

¹ But now, Job, pay attention to my speech,
and listen to all my words.
² I am going to open my mouth;
my tongue will form words on my palate.
³ My words come from my upright heart,
and my lips speak with sincerity what they know.
⁴ The Spirit of God has made me,
and the breath of the Almighty gives me life.
⁵ Refute me if you can.
Prepare your case against me; take your stand.
⁶ I am just like you before God;
I was also pinched off from a piece of clay.
⁷ Fear of me should not terrify you;
no pressure from me should weigh you down.

⁸ Surely you have spoken in my hearing,
and I have heard these very words:
⁹ "I am pure, without transgression;
I am clean and have no iniquity.
¹⁰ But he finds reasons to oppose me;
he regards me as his enemy.
¹¹ He puts my feet in the stocks;
he stands watch over all my paths."

¹² But I tell you that you are wrong in this matter,
since God is greater than man.
¹³ Why do you take him to court
for not answering anything a person asks?
¹⁴ For God speaks time and again,
but a person may not notice it.
¹⁵ In a dream, a vision in the night,
when deep sleep comes over people
as they slumber on their beds,
¹⁶ he uncovers their ears
and terrifies them with warnings,
¹⁷ in order to turn a person from his actions
and suppress the pride of a person.
¹⁸ God spares his soul from the Pit,
his life from crossing the river of death.
¹⁹ A person may be disciplined on his bed with pain
and constant distress in his bones,
²⁰ so that he detests bread,
and his soul despises his favorite food.
²¹ His flesh wastes away to nothing,
and his unseen bones stick out.
²² He draws near to the Pit,
and his life to the executioners.
²³ If there is an angel on his side,
one mediator out of a thousand,
to tell a person what is right for him
²⁴ and to be gracious to him and say,
"Spare him from going down to the Pit;
I have found a ransom,"
²⁵ then his flesh will be healthier than in his youth,
and he will return to the days of his youthful vigor.
²⁶ He will pray to God, and God will delight in him.
That person will see his face with a shout of joy,
and God will restore his righteousness to him.
²⁷ He will look at men and say,
"I have sinned and perverted what was right;
yet I did not get what I deserved.
²⁸ He redeemed my soul from going down to the Pit,
and I will continue to see the light."
²⁹ God certainly does all these things
two or three times to a person

³⁰ in order to turn him back from the Pit,
so he may shine with the light of life.
³¹ Pay attention, Job, and listen to me.
Be quiet, and I will speak.
³² But if you have something to say, answer me;
speak, for I would like to justify you.
³³ If not, then listen to me;
be quiet, and I will teach you wisdom.

PSALM 118:8

It is better to take refuge in the Lord
than to trust in humanity.

MARK 12:28-31

²⁸ One of the scribes approached. When he heard them debating and saw that Jesus answered them well, he asked him, "Which command is the most important of all?"

²⁹ Jesus answered, "The most important is Listen, O Israel! The Lord our God, the Lord is one. ³⁰ Love the Lord your God with all your heart, with all your soul, with all your mind, and with all your strength. ³¹ The second is, Love your neighbor as yourself. There is no other command greater than these."

NOTES

Day 20

GRACE DAY

Use this day to pray, rest, and reflect on this week's reading.

"Where is the road to the home of light? Do you know where darkness lives, so you can lead it back to its border? Are you familiar with the paths to its home? Don't you know? You were already born; you have lived so long! Have you entered the place where the snow is stored?

JOB 38:19–24

Or have you seen the storehouses of hail, which I hold in reserve for times of trouble, for the day of warfare and battle? What road leads to the place where light is dispersed? Where is the source of the east wind that spreads across the earth?"

Day 21

Weekly

Scripture is God-breathed and true. When we memorize it, we carry the gospel with us wherever we go.

We are memorizing Job 19:25–27, Job's declaration that his hope lies in his Redeemer. This week we will memorize Job 19:26.

Find the corresponding memory card in the back of this book.

/ /
DATE

Truth

Even after my skin has been destroyed,
yet I will see God in my flesh.

JOB 19:26

Day 22

ELIHU'S APPEAL TO WISDOM

JOB 34–35, PSALM 28:1–2, PSALM 55:16–17

JOB 34

¹ Then Elihu continued, saying:

² Hear my words, you wise ones,
and listen to me, you knowledgeable ones.
³ Doesn't the ear test words
as the palate tastes food?
⁴ Let us judge for ourselves what is right;
let us decide together what is good.
⁵ For Job has declared, "I am righteous,
yet God has deprived me of justice.
⁶ Would I lie about my case?
My wound is incurable,
though I am without transgression."
⁷ What man is like Job?
He drinks derision like water.
⁸ He keeps company with evildoers
and walks with wicked men.
⁹ For he has said, "A man gains nothing
when he becomes God's friend."

¹⁰ Therefore listen to me, you men of understanding.
It is impossible for God to do wrong,
and for the Almighty to act unjustly.
¹¹ For he repays a person according to his deeds,
and he gives him what his conduct deserves.
¹² Indeed, it is true that God does not act wickedly
and the Almighty does not pervert justice.
¹³ Who gave him authority over the earth?
Who put him in charge of the entire world?
¹⁴ If he put his mind to it
and withdrew the spirit and breath he gave,
¹⁵ every living thing would perish together
and mankind would return to the dust.

¹⁶ If you have understanding, hear this;
listen to what I have to say.
¹⁷ Could one who hates justice govern the world?
Will you condemn the mighty Righteous One,
¹⁸ who says to a king, "Worthless man!"
and to nobles, "Wicked men!"?

[19] God is not partial to princes
and does not favor the rich over the poor,
for they are all the work of his hands.
[20] They die suddenly in the middle of the night;
people shudder, then pass away.
Even the mighty are removed without effort.

[21] For his eyes watch over a man's ways,
and he observes all his steps.
[22] There is no darkness, no deep darkness,
where evildoers can hide.
[23] God does not need to examine a person further,
that one should approach him in court.
[24] He shatters the mighty without an investigation
and sets others in their place.
[25] Therefore, he recognizes their deeds
and overthrows them by night, and they are crushed.
[26] In full view of the public,
he strikes them for their wickedness,
[27] because they turned aside from following him
and did not understand any of his ways
[28] but caused the poor to cry out to him,
and he heard the outcry of the needy.
[29] But when God is silent, who can declare him guilty?
When he hides his face, who can see him?
Yet he watches over both individuals and nations,
[30] so that godless men should not rule
or ensnare the people.

[31] Suppose someone says to God,
"I have endured my punishment;
I will no longer act wickedly.
[32] Teach me what I cannot see;
if I have done wrong, I won't do it again."
[33] Should God repay you on your terms
when you have rejected his?
You must choose, not I!
So declare what you know.
[34] Reasonable men will say to me,
along with the wise men who hear me,
[35] "Job speaks without knowledge;
his words are without insight."

³⁶ If only Job were tested to the limit,
because his answers are like those of wicked men.
³⁷ For he adds rebellion to his sin;
he scornfully claps in our presence,
while multiplying his words against God.

JOB 35

¹ Then Elihu continued, saying:

² Do you think it is just when you say,
"I am righteous before God"?
³ For you ask, "What does it profit you,
and what benefit comes to me, if I do not sin?"
⁴ I will answer you
and your friends with you.
⁵ Look at the heavens and see;
gaze at the clouds high above you.
⁶ If you sin, how does it affect God?
If you multiply your transgressions, what does it do to him?
⁷ If you are righteous, what do you give him,
or what does he receive from your hand?
⁸ Your wickedness affects a person like yourself,
and your righteousness, a son of man.
⁹ People cry out because of severe oppression;
they shout for help because of the power of the mighty.
¹⁰ But no one asks, "Where is God my Maker,
who provides us with songs in the night,
¹¹ who gives us more understanding than the animals of the earth
and makes us wiser than the birds of the sky?"
¹² There they cry out, but he does not answer,
because of the pride of evil people.
¹³ Indeed, God does not listen to empty cries,
and the Almighty does not take note of it—
¹⁴ how much less when you complain
that you do not see him,
that your case is before him
and you are waiting for him.
¹⁵ But now, because God's anger does not punish
and he does not pay attention to transgression,
¹⁶ Job opens his mouth in vain
and multiplies words without knowledge.

PSALM 28:1-2

MY STRENGTH

Of David.

¹ LORD, I call to you;
my rock, do not be deaf to me.
If you remain silent to me,
I will be like those going down to the Pit.
² Listen to the sound of my pleading
when I cry to you for help,
when I lift up my hands
toward your holy sanctuary.

PSALM 55:16-17

¹⁶ But I call to God,
and the LORD will save me.
¹⁷ I complain and groan morning, noon, and night,
and he hears my voice.

NOTES

Day 23

THE MERCY AND MAJESTY OF GOD

JOB 36–37, JEREMIAH 9:24, ROMANS 5:20–21

JOB 36

¹ Then Elihu continued, saying:

² Be patient with me a little longer, and I will inform you,
for there is still more to be said on God's behalf.
³ I will get my knowledge from a distant place
and ascribe justice to my Maker.
⁴ Indeed, my words are not false;
one who has complete knowledge is with you.

⁵ Yes, God is mighty, but he despises no one;
he understands all things.
⁶ He does not keep the wicked alive,
but he gives justice to the oppressed.
⁷ He does not withdraw his gaze from the righteous,
but he seats them forever with enthroned kings,
and they are exalted.

⁸ If people are bound with chains
and trapped by the cords of affliction,
⁹ God tells them what they have done
and how arrogantly they have transgressed.
¹⁰ He opens their ears to correction
and tells them to repent from iniquity.
¹¹ If they listen and serve him,
they will end their days in prosperity
and their years in happiness.
¹² But if they do not listen,
they will cross the river of death
and die without knowledge.

¹³ Those who have a godless heart harbor anger;
even when God binds them, they do not cry for help.
¹⁴ They die in their youth;
their life ends among male cult prostitutes.
¹⁵ God rescues the afflicted by their affliction;
he instructs them by their torment.

¹⁶ Indeed, he lured you from the jaws of distress
to a spacious and unconfined place.
Your table was spread with choice food.

¹⁷ Yet now you are obsessed with the judgment due the wicked;
judgment and justice have seized you.
¹⁸ Be careful that no one lures you with riches;
do not let a large ransom lead you astray.
¹⁹ Can your wealth or all your physical exertion
keep you from distress?
²⁰ Do not long for the night
when nations will disappear from their places.
²¹ Be careful that you do not turn to iniquity,
for that is why you have been tested by affliction.

²² Look, God shows himself exalted by his power.
Who is a teacher like him?
²³ Who has appointed his way for him,
and who has declared, "You have done wrong"?
²⁴ Remember that you should praise his work,
which people have sung about.
²⁵ All mankind has seen it;
people have looked at it from a distance.
²⁶ Yes, God is exalted beyond our knowledge;
the number of his years cannot be counted.
²⁷ For he makes waterdrops evaporate;
they distill the rain into its mist,
²⁸ which the clouds pour out
and shower abundantly on mankind.
²⁹ Can anyone understand how the clouds spread out
or how the thunder roars from God's pavilion?
³⁰ See how he spreads his lightning around him
and covers the depths of the sea.
³¹ For he judges the nations with these;
he gives food in abundance.
³² He covers his hands with lightning
and commands it to hit its mark.
³³ The thunder declares his presence;
the cattle also, the approaching storm.

JOB 37

¹ My heart pounds at this
and leaps from my chest.
² Just listen to his thunderous voice
and the rumbling that comes from his mouth.

³ He lets it loose beneath the entire sky;
his lightning to the ends of the earth.

⁴ Then there comes a roaring sound;
God thunders with his majestic voice.
He does not restrain the lightning
when his rumbling voice is heard.
⁵ God thunders wondrously with his voice;
he does great things that we cannot comprehend.
⁶ For he says to the snow, "Fall to the earth,"
and the torrential rains, his mighty torrential rains,
⁷ serve as his sign to all mankind,
so that all men may know his work.
⁸ The wild animals enter their lairs
and stay in their dens.
⁹ The windstorm comes from its chamber,
and the cold from the driving north winds.
¹⁰ Ice is formed by the breath of God,
and watery expanses are frozen.
¹¹ He saturates clouds with moisture;
he scatters his lightning through them.
¹² They swirl about,
turning round and round at his direction,
accomplishing everything he commands them
over the surface of the inhabited world.
¹³ He causes this to happen for punishment,
for his land, or for his faithful love.

¹⁴ Listen to this, Job.
Stop and consider God's wonders.
¹⁵ Do you know how God directs his clouds
or makes their lightning flash?
¹⁶ Do you understand how the clouds float,
those wonderful works of him who has perfect knowledge?
¹⁷ You whose clothes get hot
when the south wind brings calm to the land,
¹⁸ can you help God spread out the skies
as hard as a cast metal mirror?
¹⁹ Teach us what we should say to him;
we cannot prepare our case because of our darkness.
²⁰ Should he be told that I want to speak?
Can a man speak when he is confused?

²¹ Now no one can even look at the sun
when it is in the skies,
after a wind has swept through and cleared the clouds away.
²² Yet out of the north he comes, shrouded in a golden glow;
awesome majesty surrounds him.
²³ The Almighty—we cannot reach him—
he is exalted in power!
He will not violate justice and abundant righteousness,
²⁴ therefore, men fear him.
He does not look favorably on any who are wise in heart.

JEREMIAH 9:24

"But the one who boasts should boast in this:
that he understands and knows me—
that I am the Lord, showing faithful love,
justice, and righteousness on the earth,
for I delight in these things.
   This is the Lord's declaration."

ROMANS 5:20-21

²⁰ The law came along to multiply the trespass. But where sin multiplied, grace multiplied even more ²¹ so that, just as sin reigned in death, so also grace will reign through righteousness, resulting in eternal life through Jesus Christ our Lord.

NOTES

Day 24

GOD'S FIRST SPEECH

JOB 38–39, JEREMIAH 31:35–36, REVELATION 3:14–20

JOB 38

THE LORD SPEAKS

¹ Then the L ORD answered Job from the whirlwind. He said:

² Who is this who obscures my counsel
with ignorant words?
³ Get ready to answer me like a man;
when I question you, you will inform me.
⁴ Where were you when I established the earth?
Tell me, if you have understanding.
⁵ Who fixed its dimensions? Certainly you know!
Who stretched a measuring line across it?
⁶ What supports its foundations?
Or who laid its cornerstone
⁷ while the morning stars sang together
and all the sons of God shouted for joy?

⁸ Who enclosed the sea behind doors
when it burst from the womb,
⁹ when I made the clouds its garment
and total darkness its blanket,
¹⁰ when I determined its boundaries
and put its bars and doors in place,
¹¹ when I declared: "You may come this far, but no farther;
your proud waves stop here"?

¹² Have you ever in your life commanded the morning
or assigned the dawn its place,
¹³ so it may seize the edges of the earth
and shake the wicked out of it?
¹⁴ The earth is changed as clay is by a seal;
its hills stand out like the folds of a garment.
¹⁵ Light is withheld from the wicked,
and the arm raised in violence is broken.

¹⁶ Have you traveled to the sources of the sea
or walked in the depths of the oceans?
¹⁷ Have the gates of death been revealed to you?
Have you seen the gates of deep darkness?
¹⁸ Have you comprehended the extent of the earth?
Tell me, if you know all this.

[19] Where is the road to the home of light?
Do you know where darkness lives,
[20] so you can lead it back to its border?
Are you familiar with the paths to its home?
[21] Don't you know? You were already born;
you have lived so long!
[22] Have you entered the place where the snow is stored?
Or have you seen the storehouses of hail,
[23] which I hold in reserve for times of trouble,
for the day of warfare and battle?
[24] What road leads to the place where light is dispersed?
Where is the source of the east wind that spreads across the earth?

[25] Who cuts a channel for the flooding rain
or clears the way for lightning,
[26] to bring rain on an uninhabited land,
on a desert with no human life,
[27] to satisfy the parched wasteland
and cause the grass to sprout?
[28] Does the rain have a father?
Who fathered the drops of dew?
[29] Whose womb did the ice come from?
Who gave birth to the frost of heaven
[30] when water becomes as hard as stone,
and the surface of the watery depths is frozen?

[31] Can you fasten the chains of the Pleiades
or loosen the belt of Orion?
[32] Can you bring out the constellations in their season
and lead the Bear and her cubs?
[33] Do you know the laws of heaven?
Can you impose its authority on earth?
[34] Can you command the clouds
so that a flood of water covers you?
[35] Can you send out lightning bolts, and they go?
Do they report to you: "Here we are"?

[36] Who put wisdom in the heart
or gave the mind understanding?
[37] Who has the wisdom to number the clouds?
Or who can tilt the water jars of heaven

⁳⁸ when the dust hardens like cast metal
and the clods of dirt stick together?

³⁹ Can you hunt prey for a lioness
or satisfy the appetite of young lions
⁴⁰ when they crouch in their dens
and lie in wait within their lairs?
⁴¹ Who provides the raven's food
when its young cry out to God
and wander about for lack of food?

JOB 39

¹ Do you know when mountain goats give birth?
Have you watched the deer in labor?
² Can you count the months they are pregnant
so you can know the time they give birth?
³ They crouch down to give birth to their young;
they deliver their newborn.
⁴ Their offspring are healthy and grow up in the open field.
They leave and do not return.

⁵ Who set the wild donkey free?
Who released the swift donkey from its harness?
⁶ I made the desert its home,
and the salty wasteland its dwelling.
⁷ It scoffs at the noise of the village
and never hears the shouts of a driver.
⁸ It roams the mountains for its pastureland,
searching for anything green.
⁹ Would the wild ox be willing to serve you?
Would it spend the night by your feeding trough?
¹⁰ Can you hold the wild ox to a furrow by its harness?
Will it plow the valleys behind you?
¹¹ Can you depend on it because its strength is great?
Would you leave it to do your hard work?
¹² Can you trust the wild ox to harvest your grain
and bring it to your threshing floor?

¹³ The wings of the ostrich flap joyfully,
but are her feathers and plumage like the stork's?
¹⁴ She abandons her eggs on the ground
and lets them be warmed in the sand.
¹⁵ She forgets that a foot may crush them
or that some wild animal may trample them.
¹⁶ She treats her young harshly, as if they were not her own,
with no fear that her labor may have been in vain.
¹⁷ For God has deprived her of wisdom;
he has not endowed her with understanding.
¹⁸ When she proudly spreads her wings,
she laughs at the horse and its rider.

¹⁹ Do you give strength to the horse?
Do you adorn his neck with a mane?
²⁰ Do you make him leap like a locust?
His proud snorting fills one with terror.
²¹ He paws in the valley and rejoices in his strength;
he charges into battle.
²² He laughs at fear, since he is afraid of nothing;
he does not run from the sword.
²³ A quiver rattles at his side,
along with a flashing spear and a javelin.
²⁴ He charges ahead with trembling rage;
he cannot stand still at the trumpet's sound.
²⁵ When the trumpet blasts, he snorts defiantly.
He smells the battle from a distance;
he hears the officers' shouts and the battle cry.

²⁶ Does the hawk take flight by your understanding
and spread its wings to the south?
²⁷ Does the eagle soar at your command
and make its nest on high?
²⁸ It lives on a cliff where it spends the night;
its stronghold is on a rocky crag.
²⁹ From there it searches for prey;
its eyes penetrate the distance.
³⁰ Its brood gulps down blood,
and where the slain are, it is there.

JEREMIAH 31:35-36

³⁵ "This is what the LORD says:

> The one who gives the sun for light by day,
> the fixed order of moon and stars for light
>   by night,
> who stirs up the sea and makes its
>   waves roar—
> the LORD of Armies is his name:
> ³⁶ If this fixed order departs from
>   before me—
>   this is the LORD's declaration—
> only then will Israel's descendants cease
> to be a nation before me forever."

REVELATION 3:14-20

THE LETTER TO LAODICEA

¹⁴ "Write to the angel of the church in Laodicea:

Thus says the Amen, the faithful and true witness, the originator of God's creation: ¹⁵ I know your works, that you are neither cold nor hot. I wish that you were cold or hot. ¹⁶ So, because you are lukewarm, and neither hot nor cold, I am going to vomit you out of my mouth. ¹⁷ For you say, 'I'm rich; I have become wealthy and need nothing,' and you don't realize that you are wretched, pitiful, poor, blind, and naked. ¹⁸ I advise you to buy from me gold refined in the fire so that you may be rich, white clothes so that you may be dressed and your shameful nakedness not be exposed, and ointment to spread on your eyes so that you may see. ¹⁹ As many as I love, I rebuke and discipline. So be zealous and repent. ²⁰ See! I stand at the door and knock. If anyone hears my voice and opens the door, I will come in to him and eat with him, and he with me."

NOTES

Asked in Job, Answered in Jesus

The Old Testament book of Job shares an intimate connection with the New Testament. Job's weightiest questions are perfectly answered in the person of Jesus Christ.

ASKED IN JOB

Job 9:32-33	Who can help us approach God?
Job 14:14	Is there life after death?
Job 16:19-21	Is there anyone in heaven working on our behalf?
Job 21:15	What is the value of knowing God?
Job 23:3-5	Where do we find God?

ANSWERED IN JESUS

For there is one God and one mediator between God and humanity, the man Christ Jesus.

1Tm 2:5

"I am the resurrection and the life. The one who believes in me, even if he dies, will live."

Jn 11:25

Christ Jesus is the one who died, but even more, has been raised; he also is at the right hand of God and intercedes for us.

Rm 8:34

"For God loved the world in this way: He gave his one and only Son, so that everyone who believes in him will not perish but have eternal life."

Jn 3:16

"The one who has seen me has seen the Father."

Jn 14:9

Day 25

GOD'S SECOND SPEECH

JOB 40–41, MARK 4:35–41, JAMES 1:5–8

JOB 40

¹ The Lord answered Job:

² Will the one who contends with the Almighty correct him?
Let him who argues with God give an answer.

³ Then Job answered the Lord:

⁴ I am so insignificant. How can I answer you?
I place my hand over my mouth.
⁵ I have spoken once, and I will not reply;
twice, but now I can add nothing.

⁶ Then the Lord answered Job from the whirlwind:

⁷ Get ready to answer me like a man;
When I question you, you will inform me.
⁸ Would you really challenge my justice?
Would you declare me guilty to justify yourself?
⁹ Do you have an arm like God's?
Can you thunder with a voice like his?

¹⁰ Adorn yourself with majesty and splendor,
and clothe yourself with honor and glory.
¹¹ Pour out your raging anger;
look on every proud person and humiliate him.
¹² Look on every proud person and humble him;
trample the wicked where they stand.
¹³ Hide them together in the dust;
imprison them in the grave.
¹⁴ Then I will confess to you
that your own right hand can deliver you.

¹⁵ Look at Behemoth,
which I made along with you.
He eats grass like cattle.
¹⁶ Look at the strength of his back
and the power in the muscles of his belly.
¹⁷ He stiffens his tail like a cedar tree;
the tendons of his thighs are woven firmly together.
¹⁸ His bones are bronze tubes;
his limbs are like iron rods.

¹⁹ He is the foremost of God's works;
only his Maker can draw the sword against him.
²⁰ The hills yield food for him,
while all sorts of wild animals play there.
²¹ He lies under the lotus plants,
hiding in the protection of marshy reeds.
²² Lotus plants cover him with their shade;
the willows by the brook surround him.
²³ Though the river rages, Behemoth is unafraid;
he remains confident, even if the Jordan surges up to his mouth.
²⁴ Can anyone capture him while he looks on,
or pierce his nose with snares?

JOB 41

¹ Can you pull in Leviathan with a hook
or tie his tongue down with a rope?
² Can you put a cord through his nose
or pierce his jaw with a hook?
³ Will he beg you for mercy
or speak softly to you?
⁴ Will he make a covenant with you
so that you can take him as a slave forever?
⁵ Can you play with him like a bird
or put him on a leash for your girls?
⁶ Will traders bargain for him
or divide him among the merchants?
⁷ Can you fill his hide with harpoons
or his head with fishing spears?
⁸ Lay a hand on him.
You will remember the battle
and never repeat it!
⁹ Any hope of capturing him proves false.
Does a person not collapse at the very sight of him?
¹⁰ No one is ferocious enough to rouse Leviathan;
who then can stand against me?
¹¹ Who confronted me, that I should repay him?
Everything under heaven belongs to me.

¹² I cannot be silent about his limbs,
his power, and his graceful proportions.

¹³ Who can strip off his outer covering?
Who can penetrate his double layer of armor?
¹⁴ Who can open his jaws,
surrounded by those terrifying teeth?
¹⁵ His pride is in his rows of scales,
closely sealed together.
¹⁶ One scale is so close to another
that no air can pass between them.
¹⁷ They are joined to one another,
so closely connected they cannot be separated.
¹⁸ His snorting flashes with light,
while his eyes are like the rays of dawn.
¹⁹ Flaming torches shoot from his mouth;
fiery sparks fly out!
²⁰ Smoke billows from his nostrils
as from a boiling pot or burning reeds.
²¹ His breath sets coals ablaze,
and flames pour out of his mouth.
²² Strength resides in his neck,
and dismay dances before him.
²³ The folds of his flesh are joined together,
solid as metal and immovable.
²⁴ His heart is as hard as a rock,
as hard as a lower millstone!
²⁵ When Leviathan rises, the mighty are terrified;
they withdraw because of his thrashing.
²⁶ The sword that reaches him will have no effect,
nor will a spear, dart, or arrow.
²⁷ He regards iron as straw,
and bronze as rotten wood.
²⁸ No arrow can make him flee;
slingstones become like stubble to him.
²⁹ A club is regarded as stubble,
and he laughs at the sound of a javelin.
³⁰ His undersides are jagged potsherds,
spreading the mud like a threshing sledge.
³¹ He makes the depths seethe like a cauldron;
he makes the sea like an ointment jar.
³² He leaves a shining wake behind him;
one would think the deep had gray hair!
³³ He has no equal on earth—
a creature devoid of fear!

³⁴ He surveys everything that is haughty;
he is king over all the proud beasts.

MARK 4:35-41

WIND AND WAVES OBEY JESUS

³⁵ On that day, when evening had come, he told them, "Let's cross over to the other side of the sea." ³⁶ So they left the crowd and took him along since he was in the boat. And other boats were with him. ³⁷ A great windstorm arose, and the waves were breaking over the boat, so that the boat was already being swamped. ³⁸ He was in the stern, sleeping on the cushion. So they woke him up and said to him, "Teacher! Don't you care that we're going to die?"

³⁹ He got up, rebuked the wind, and said to the sea, "Silence! Be still!" The wind ceased, and there was a great calm. ⁴⁰ Then he said to them, "Why are you afraid? Do you still have no faith?"

⁴¹ And they were terrified and asked one another, "Who then is this? Even the wind and the sea obey him!"

JAMES 1:5-8

⁵ Now if any of you lacks wisdom, he should ask God—who gives to all generously and ungrudgingly—and it will be given to him. ⁶ But let him ask in faith without doubting. For the doubter is like the surging sea, driven and tossed by the wind. ⁷ That person should not expect to receive anything from the Lord, ⁸ being double-minded and unstable in all his ways.

NOTES

Day 26

THE RESTORATION OF JOB

JOB 42, PSALM 40:10–13, LAMENTATIONS 3:19–26

JOB 42

JOB REPLIES TO THE LORD

¹ Then Job replied to the Lord:

² I know that you can do anything
and no plan of yours can be thwarted.
³ You asked, "Who is this who conceals my
counsel with ignorance?"
Surely I spoke about things I did not
understand,
things too wondrous for me to know.
⁴ You said, "Listen now, and I will speak.
When I question you, you will inform me."
⁵ I had heard reports about you,
but now my eyes have seen you.
⁶ Therefore, I reject my words and am sorry
for them;
I am dust and ashes.

⁷ After the Lord had finished speaking to Job, he said to Eliphaz the Temanite: "I am angry with you and your two friends, for you have not spoken the truth about me, as my servant Job has. ⁸ Now take seven bulls and seven rams, go to my servant Job, and offer a burnt offering for yourselves. Then my servant Job will pray for you. I will surely accept his prayer and not deal with you as your folly deserves. For you have not spoken the truth about me, as my servant Job has." ⁹ Then Eliphaz the Temanite, Bildad the Shuhite, and Zophar the Naamathite went and did as the Lord had told them, and the Lord accepted Job's prayer.

GOD RESTORES JOB

¹⁰ After Job had prayed for his friends, the Lord restored his fortunes and doubled his previous possessions. ¹¹ All his brothers, sisters, and former acquaintances came to him and dined with him in his house. They sympathized with him and comforted him concerning all the adversity the Lord had brought on him. Each one gave him a piece of silver and a gold earring.

¹² So the Lord blessed the last part of Job's life more than the first. He owned fourteen thousand sheep and goats, six thousand camels, one thousand yoke of oxen, and one thousand female donkeys. ¹³ He also had seven sons and three daughters. ¹⁴ He named his first daughter Jemimah, his second Keziah, and his third Keren-happuch. ¹⁵ No women as beautiful as Job's daughters could be found in all the land, and their father granted them an inheritance with their brothers.

¹⁶ Job lived 140 years after this and saw his children and their children to the fourth generation. ¹⁷ Then Job died, old and full of days.

PSALM 40:10-13

¹⁰ I did not hide your righteousness in my heart;
I spoke about your faithfulness and salvation;
I did not conceal your constant love and truth
from the great assembly.

¹¹ Lord, you do not withhold your
compassion from me.
Your constant love and truth will always
guard me.
¹² For troubles without number have
surrounded me;
my iniquities have overtaken me; I am unable
to see.
They are more than the hairs of my head,
and my courage leaves me.
¹³ Lord, be pleased to rescue me;
hurry to help me, Lord.

LAMENTATIONS 3:19-26

ז ZAYIN

[19] Remember my affliction and my homelessness,
the wormwood and the poison.
[20] I continually remember them
and have become depressed.
[21] Yet I call this to mind,
and therefore I have hope:

ח CHETH

[22] Because of the Lord's faithful love
we do not perish,
for his mercies never end.
[23] They are new every morning;
great is your faithfulness!
[24] I say, "The Lord is my portion,
therefore I will put my hope in him."

ט TETH

[25] The Lord is good to those who wait for him,
to the person who seeks him.
[26] It is good to wait quietly
for salvation from the Lord.

NOTES

Day 27

GRACE DAY

Use this day to pray, rest, and reflect on this week's reading.

"Can you fasten the chains of the Pleiades or loosen the belt of Orion? Can you bring out the constellations in their season and lead the Bear and her cubs? Do you know the laws of heaven?

JOB 38:31–35

Can you impose its authority on earth? Can you command the clouds so that a flood of water covers you? Can you send out lightning bolts, and they go? Do they report to you: 'Here we are'?"

Day 28

Weekly

Scripture is God-breathed and true. When we memorize it, we carry the gospel with us wherever we go.

This week we will memorize the last verse of Job 19:25–27, Job's declaration that his hope lies in his Redeemer.

Find the corresponding memory card in the back of this book.

DATE

Truth

I will see him myself;
my eyes will look at him,
and not as a stranger.
My heart longs within me.

JOB 19:27

Study Questions

*Use this section for personal study, or
gather some friends and neighbors to
discuss these questions together.*

Week 1

STUDY QUESTIONS

JOB 2:11-13

JOB'S THREE FRIENDS

¹¹ Now when Job's three friends heard of all these troubles that had come upon him, each of them set out from his home—Eliphaz the Temanite, Bildad the Shuhite, and Zophar the Naamathite. They met together to go and console and comfort him. ¹² When they saw him from a distance, they did not recognize him, and they raised their voices and wept aloud; they tore their robes and threw dust in the air upon their heads. ¹³ They sat with him on the ground seven days and seven nights, and no one spoke a word to him, for they saw that his suffering was very great.

01 How did Job's friends react to his troubles?

02 Why is it important for us to share our burdens with the people around us?

03 Have you had friends who have reacted poorly when you shared information about hard times with them? What is your ideal response from people close to you in times of hardship?

Week 2

STUDY QUESTIONS

JOB 12:1-6

JOB'S REPLY TO ZOPHAR

¹ Then Job answered:

² No doubt you are the people,
and wisdom will die with you!
³ But I also have a mind like you;
I am not inferior to you.
Who doesn't know the things you are talking about?

⁴ I am a laughingstock to my friends,
by calling on God, who answers me.
The righteous and upright man is a laughingstock.
⁵ The one who is at ease holds calamity in contempt
and thinks it is prepared for those whose feet are slipping.
⁶ The tents of robbers are safe,
and those who trouble God are secure;
God holds them in his hands.

01 Why was Job considered a laughingstock?

02 Have you ever had someone you trust give you bad advice?

03 Put yourself in the position of Job's friends. Have you tried to give your friends advice and had it turn out to be more harmful than helpful?

Week 3

STUDY QUESTIONS

JOB 23:1-12

¹ Then Job answered:

² Today also my complaint is bitter.
His hand is heavy despite my groaning.
³ If only I knew how to find him,
so that I could go to his throne.
⁴ I would plead my case before him
and fill my mouth with arguments.
⁵ I would learn how he would answer me;
and understand what he would say to me.
⁶ Would he prosecute me forcefully?
No, he would certainly pay attention
 to me.
⁷ Then an upright man could reason
 with him,
and I would escape from my Judge forever.
⁸ If I go east, he is not there,
and if I go west, I cannot perceive him.
⁹ When he is at work to the north, I cannot
 see him;
when he turns south, I cannot find him.
¹⁰ Yet he knows the way I have taken;
when he has tested me, I will emerge as
 pure gold.
¹¹ My feet have followed in his tracks;
I have kept to his way and not turned aside.
¹² I have not departed from the commands
 from his lips;
I have treasured the words from his mouth
more than my daily food.

01 How does Job try to justify his attitude toward God?

02 Describe a time where you felt like you couldn't find God, like Job in verses 8–9.

03 Job says that he will "emerge as pure gold" (v. 10) after God has tested him. How have you seen God refine you throughout your life?

Week 4

STUDY QUESTIONS

JOB 38:1-11

THE LORD SPEAKS

¹ Then the LORD answered Job from the whirlwind. He said:

² Who is this who obscures my counsel
with ignorant words?
³ Get ready to answer me like a man;
when I question you, you will inform me.
⁴ Where were you when I established the
   earth?
Tell me, if you have understanding.
⁵ Who fixed its dimensions? Certainly
   you know!
Who stretched a measuring line across it?
⁶ What supports its foundations?
Or who laid its cornerstone
⁷ while the morning stars sang together
and all the sons of God shouted for joy?
⁸ Who enclosed the sea behind doors
when it burst from the womb,
⁹ when I made the clouds its garment
and total darkness its blanket,
¹⁰ when I determined its boundaries
and put its bars and doors in place,
¹¹ when I declared: "You may come this far,
   but no farther;
your proud waves stop here"?

01 How does God rebuke Job's friends? Why does He do this?

02 When God speaks to Job about Himself, what does He reveal about His power?

03 When do you need to be reminded of who God is?

DOWNLOAD THE APP

STOP BY
hereadstruth.com

SHOP
shophereadstruth.com

SEND A NOTE
hello@hereadstruth.com

SHARE
#HeReadsTruth

BIBLIOGRAPHY

Bartholomew, Craig G. "Wisdom Literature" in *Faithlife Study Bible*. Bellingham, WA: Lexham Press, 2012, 2016.

HE READS TRUTH

MEN IN THE WORD OF GOD EVERY DAY.

He Reads Truth is a community of men who read God's Word together every day. We help men engage with Scripture through daily Bible reading plans, online essays about each day's reading, and printed resources designed for deeper engagement. Start reading along today.

@hereadstruth | hereadstruth.com

FOR THE RECORD

Where did I study?

- [ ] HOME
- [ ] OFFICE
- [ ] CHURCH
- [ ] SCHOOL
- [ ] COFFEE SHOP
- [ ] OTHER:

_____

_____

WHAT WAS I LISTENING TO?

Song: _____

Artist: _____

Album: _____

_____

What time of day did I study?

- [ ] MORNING
- [ ] AFTERNOON
- [ ] NIGHT
- [ ] OTHER:

_____

_____

What was happening in the world?

_____

_____

_____

_____

What was happening in my life?

_____

_____

_____

_____

_____

_____

MY CLOSING PRAYER:

_____

END DATE

_____ / _____ / _____